CLA. . . lus

Connect

A blended solution from
Heinemann and Electric Paper

Nicola Bowman

Heinemann
Inspiring generations

Heinemann Educational Publishers
Halley Court, Jordan Hill, Oxford OX2 8EJ
Part of Harcourt Education

Heinemann is the registered trademark of
Harcourt Education Limited

First published 2004

09 08 07 06 05 04
10 9 8 7 6 5 4 3 2 1

British Library Cataloguing in Publication Data is available
from the British Library on request.

ISBN 0 435 45057 3

Typeset by P.K. McBride, Southampton

Cover design by Wooden Ark Studio

Printed in Great Britain by Bath Press.

Cover photo: © Digital Vision

Acknowledgements
Every effort has been made to contact copyright holders of material reproduced in this book. Any omissions will be rectified in subsequent printings if notice is given to the publishers.

Websites
Please note that the examples of websites suggested in this book were up to date at the time of writing. It is essential for tutors to preview each site before using it to ensure that the URL is still accurate and the content is appropriate. We suggest that tutors bookmark useful sites and consider enabling students to access them through the school or college intranet.

Screenshots reprinted with permission from Microsoft Corporation.

Contents

Introduction ... vii

Unit 1: Create, manage and integrate files 1

Looking at the Desktop ... 2
- Revision: Skill Builder 1.1 ... 2

Working with Windows Explorer ... 3
- Revision: Skill Builder 1.2 ... 3
- Organising files and folders: Skill Builder 1.3 ... 4

Getting started with word processing ... 5
- Microsoft Word menus and toolbars ... 5
- Opening documents: Skill Builder 1.4 ... 6
- Saving files: Skill Builder 1.5 ... 7

Entering and editing text ... 8
- Moving and duplicating text: Skill Builder 1.6 ... 8
- Checking spelling and grammar: Skill Builder 1.7 ... 10
- Finding and replacing text: Skill Builder 1.8 ... 11

Changing the look of documents ... 12
- Styles and house styles: Skill Builder 1.9 ... 12
- Line spacing and bullets: Skill Builder 1.10 ... 13
- Using paragraphs, line breaks and styles: Skill Builder 1.11 ... 14
- Symbols: Skill Builder 1.12 ... 16

Structuring your documents ... 17
- Pages and Page Setup: Skill Builder 1.13 ... 17
- Mini Assignment 1.1 ... 18

Borders and tables ... 21
- Creating tables: Skill Builder 1.14 ... 21
- Rearranging tables: Skill Builder 1.15 ... 23
- Changing the look of tables: Skill Builder 1.16 ... 24
- Borders and tables: Skill Builder 1.17 ... 25

Working with graphics and data objects ... 26
- Modifying graphics: Skill Builder 1.18 ... 26

Publishing your work ... 27
- Printing documents: Skill Builder 1.19 ... 27
- Mini Assignment 1.2 ... 31

Units 2, 9, 10: Spreadsheets ... 33

Basic concepts ... 34
- Revision: Skill Builder 2.1 ... 34

Entering and formatting data ... 35
Creating a workbook: Skill Builder 2.2 ... 35
Advanced formatting: Skill Builder 2.3 ... 37
Mini Assignment 2.1 ... 38
Basic formulas and functions ... 39
Entering simple formulas: Skill Builder 2.4 ... 39
Combining operators in functions: Skill Builder 2.5 ... 40
Using the Function Wizard: Skill Builder 2.6 ... 41
Entering and organising data ... 42
Moving, duplicating and copying data: Skill Builder 2.7 ... 42
Deleting and inserting cells, rows and columns: Skill Builder 2.8 ... 43
Sorting data: Skill Builder 2.9 ... 44
Mini Assignment 2.2 ... 45
Charts ... 46
Types of charts ... 46
Using the Chart Wizard: Skill Builder 2.10 ... 47
Exploded pie charts ... 48
Working with the Chart toolbar: Skill Builders 2.11 & 2.12 ... 49
Formatting individual parts of a chart: Skill Builder 2.13 ... 50
Manipulating charts: Skill Builder 2.14 ... 52
Working with scatter graphs: Skill Builder 2.15 ... 53
XY (scatter) graph options ... 54
Mini Assignment 2.3 ... 55
Customising worksheets ... 56
Naming cells and ranges: Skill Builder 2.16 ... 56
Hiding spreadsheet data: Skill Builder 2.17 ... 57
Advanced formulas and functions ... 58
Relative and absolute cell address: Skill Builder 2.18 ... 58
Cell references and formulas: Skill Builder 2.19 ... 59
The IF function: Skill Builder 2.20 ... 60
Projected results: Skill Builder 2.21 ... 61
Mini Assignment 2.4 ... 62
Distributing your worksheets ... 63
Page Setup and printing: Skill Builder 2.22 ... 63
Units 3 and 11: Databases ... 65
Getting started ... 66
Database concepts: Skill Builder 3.1 ... 66
Setting up a database ... 67
Creating a new table: Skill Builder 3.2 ... 67
Introducing field properties: Skill Builder 3.3 ... 68
Working with tables ... 69
Adding data to a table: Skill Builder 3.4 ... 69
Modifying a table: Skill Builder 3.5 ... 71
Mini Assignment 3.1 ... 72

Working with forms ... 74
Database forms: Skill Builder 3.6 ... 74
Sorting records in a database ... 75
Sorting records in a table: Skill Builder 3.7 ... 75
Locating data: Skill Builder 3.8 ... 76
Working with queries ... 77
Creating a query: Skill Builder 3.9 ... 77
Working with operators: Skill Builder 3.10 ... 78
Using wildcards: Skill Builder 3.11 ... 79
Calculated fields: Skill Builder 3.12 ... 80
Creating reports and printing ... 81
Creating a report from a query: Skill Builder 3.13 ... 81
Making changes to a report: Skill Builder 3.14 ... 82
Introduction to printing: Skill Builder 3.15 ... 83
Creating and printing labels: Skill Builder 3.16 ... 84
Mini Assignment 3.2 ... 86

Units 5 and 13: Presentation graphics ... 89

Getting started ... 90
The PowerPoint screen and tools ... 90
Starting a new presentation: Skill Builder 5.1 ... 91
Creating text slides ... 92
Moving and duplicating text: Skill Builder 5.2 ... 92
Working in Outline view: Skill Builder 5.3 ... 93
Changing the look of slides ... 94
Design templates: Skill Builder 5.4 ... 94
Working with master slides: Skill Builder 5.5 ... 95
Adding headers and footers to slides: Skill Builder 5.6 ... 96
Adding borders and shading to a placeholder: Skill Builder: 5.7 ... 97
Mini Assignment 5.1 ... 98
Preparing on-screen presentations ... 100
Animations and transitions: Skill Builder 5.8 ... 100
Running a slide show: Skill Builder 5.9 ... 102
Timings: Skill Builder 5.10 ... 103
Linking slides: Skill Builder 5.11 ... 104
Hide a slide: Skill Builder 5.12 ... 105
Charts ... 106
Creating organisation charts: Skill Builder 5.13 ... 106
Introducing data charts: Skill Builder 5.14 ... 107
Inserting a table: Skill Builder 5.15 ... 108
Mini Assignment 5.2 ... 109
Graphics ... 111
Importing and editing graphics and Clip Art: Skill Builder 5.16 ... 111
Resizing and cropping graphics: Skill Builder 5.17 ... 112

Preparing and publishing presentations 113
Replacing text: Skill Builder 5.18 113
Creating speaker's notes: Skill Builder 5.19 114
Printing slides and screen shots: Skill Builder 5.20 115
Mini Assignment 5.3 116

Unit 8: E-communications 117

Getting started with e-mail 118
What is e-mail: Skill Builder 8.1 118
Sending and receiving messages 119
Creating and sending messages: Skill Builder 8.2 119
Replying to messages: Skill Builder 8.3 121
Sending and receiving messages: Skill Builder 8.4 122
Using personal signatures: Skill Builder 8.5 123
Sending and receiving files with e-mail: Skill Builder 8.6 124
Good practice with e-mail 126
Managing your e-mail: Skill Builder 8.7 126
Setting rules for incoming messages: Skill Builder 8.8 127
Mini Assignment 8.1 128
Using Outlook to manage your time 129
Personal information management: Skill Builder 8.9 129
Working with the Outlook calendar: Skill Builder 8.10 130
Using tasks: Skill Builder 8.11 131
Printing from Outlook 132
Printing e-mails, contact details and calendar items: Skill Builder 8.12 132
Mini Assignment 8.2 133

The Resource Bank contains:

- source files for Skill Builders, Mini Assignments and Practice Assignments
- two full Practice Assignments for:
  - Unit 1 Create, manage and integrate files
  - Unit 2 Spreadsheets
  - Unit 3 Databases
  - Unit 5 Presentation graphics
  - Unit 8 E-communications
  - Unit 9 Graphs and charts
- one open-ended task for:
  - Unit 10 Spreadsheet solutions
  - Unit 11 Database solutions
  - Unit 13 Presentation solutions

Introduction

This book is designed to be used alongside the Electric Paper e-tutor. It acts as a guide to the computer-based learning and provides summaries, tips, reminders and – most importantly – extra practice material. This is in three forms. The **Skill Builders** should be completed immediately after the related part of the e-tutor as they give practice in the aspects that have just been covered. The **Mini Assignments** help to consolidate the techniques and concepts from the previous half of the unit. The **Practice Assignments** in the Resource Bank simulate the real CLAIT Plus assignments. After students have completed these without assistance and with the minimum of errors, they should attempt the practice assignments provided by OCR as final preparation for the exam.

The book and the e-tutor

At the top of most pages in the book you will see a menu display which allows you to see easily at a glance which modules and sections of the e-tutor you are working through.

The items highlighted in **bold red** are the ones which relate to the page. Work your way through them before returning to the page and attempting the relevant Skill Builder.

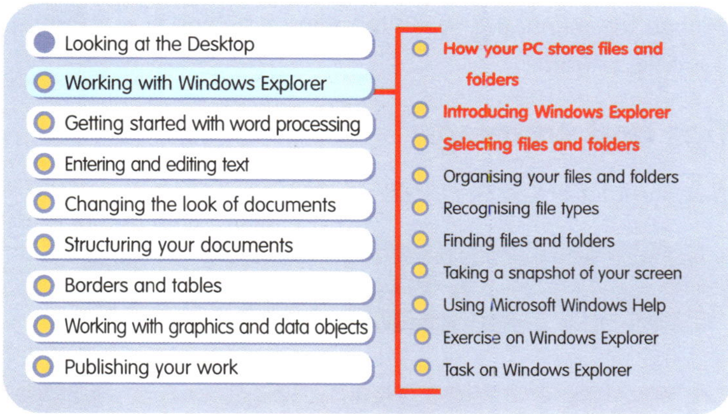

Which Windows? Which Office?

There are currently six versions of Microsoft Windows® and three versions of Microsoft Office in general use. This book has been written around Windows XP and Office XP (2002/2003). The screen displays, toolbars and menu systems shown here can be found with very slight variations in Windows 98, Me, NT and 2000, and in Office 2000. Where the differences may be enough to cause any confusion, they are pointed out. Look out for these boxes.

> In Word 2000 **File > New** opens the **New** dialogue box. The **Blank document** option is on the **General** tab.
>
> In Word 2002/2003 **File > New** opens the **New document** task pane. The **Blank document** option is in the **New** section.

There are two editions of Office XP currently in use – the original 2002 and the updated 2003. The differences are very slight, and do not affect anything at the level of this book.

Fonts and styles

Menu items, labels on buttons, headings and other key words on the screen are shown in **bold**, e.g. the **File** menu, the **OK** button.

Names of files, folders and fields in worksheets are shown in *italics*, e.g. the *tes.doc* file, *My Documents* folder.

Anything which you are asked to type is shown in Times New Roman, e.g. type the heading Deleting and replacing.

Keys are identified by [brackets], e.g. **[Insert]**. Where two or more keys must be pressed, they are linked by a + sign, e.g. **[Alt] + [F]** means hold down the **[Alt]** key and press **[F]**.

Menu commands may be presented in a short form, with > indicating the steps through the menu, e.g. 'open the **File** menu and select **Print**' may be written as 'use **File > Print**'.

Tips and warnings

Watch out for boxes like these:

This is a tip – try to remember it as it could make your life easier.

This is a warning – it tells you about things that you really must watch out for when you do the CLAIT exam.

The Resource Bank

This book is also accompanied by a Resource Bank – a CD-ROM containing the source files that are needed in the assignments and Skill Builders. The files could be copied into any convenient area of your computer or network at the start of the course, so that they can be accessed more easily when they are needed.

Practice Assignments

The Resource Bank also contains two full Practice Assignments for each unit. These are in PDF form, and can be printed as needed.

Unit 1

CREATE, MANAGE AND INTEGRATE FILES

The first unit covers file management, including how to create files and folders and to move, copy, delete and rename files and folders to ensure an efficient storage of data.

It also covers integrating files, and you will be expected to open a plain text file, add formatting to it and integrate into it a data file (e.g. a table of information), a chart (e.g. a pie or bar chart) and an image from previously created files. This document will usually be 3–4 pages in length.

In the CLAIT Plus assignment, this document usually contains deliberate spelling errors and you will be asked to search for a word and amend it to another.

- **Create, manage and integrate files**
- Spreadsheets
- Databases
- Presentation graphics
- E-communications

Throughout this unit you will be asked to open files that are supplied in the Resource Bank. They can be found on the Resource Bank CD or in the folder which your tutor may have set up for use with this course.

Looking at the Desktop

Revision

This Skill Builder covers the main skills from the whole *Looking at the Desktop* module.

- Looking at the Desktop
  - Starting your computer
  - Introducing applications
  - What are desktop icons?
  - Using desktop shortcuts
  - Introducing desktop windows
  - Using menus
  - Viewing and sorting contents in a window
  - Working with more than one window
  - Shutting down your computer
  - Exercise on Looking at the Desktop
- Working with Windows Explorer
- Getting started with word processing
- Entering and editing text
- Changing the look of documents
- Structuring your documents
- Borders and tables
- Working with graphics and data objects
- Publishing your work

Skill Builder 1.1

1. Locate the on/off switch of your PC and turn it on. If you are on a network you may have to logon using your user name and password.
2. Once you have logged on you will see the program applications on your desktop. Pick any three of those icons and write down what you would use their applications for.
3. Open *My Computer* and locate your *My Documents* folder.
4. Change the view so that the contents are displayed as a simple list.
5. Sort the files in *My Documents* into ascending order of Date Modified.
6. Close *My Documents* and *My Computer*.
7. Shut down your PC.

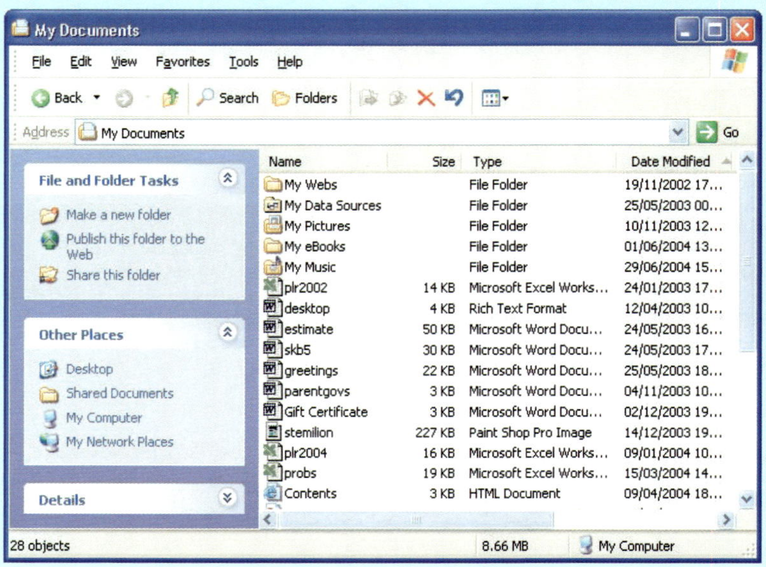

Working with Windows Explorer

Revision

A computer's hard disk is similar to a paper-based filing cabinet where each drawer can contain many folders, subfolders or documents.

- Looking at the Desktop
- Working with Windows Explorer
  - How your PC stores files and folders
  - Introducing Windows Explorer
  - Selecting files and folders
  - Organising your files and folders
  - Recognising file types
  - Finding files and folders
  - Taking a snapshot of your screen
  - Using Microsoft Windows Help
  - Exercise on Windows Explorer
  - Task on Windows Explorer
- Getting started with word processing
- Entering and editing text
- Changing the look of documents
- Structuring your documents
- Borders and tables
- Working with graphics and data objects
- Publishing your work

Skill Builder 1.2

1 Create a new folder in *My Documents* folder named *epclaitplus*.

2 Create a subfolder of *epclaitplus* and name this *builders*.

Your solution should be similar to this.

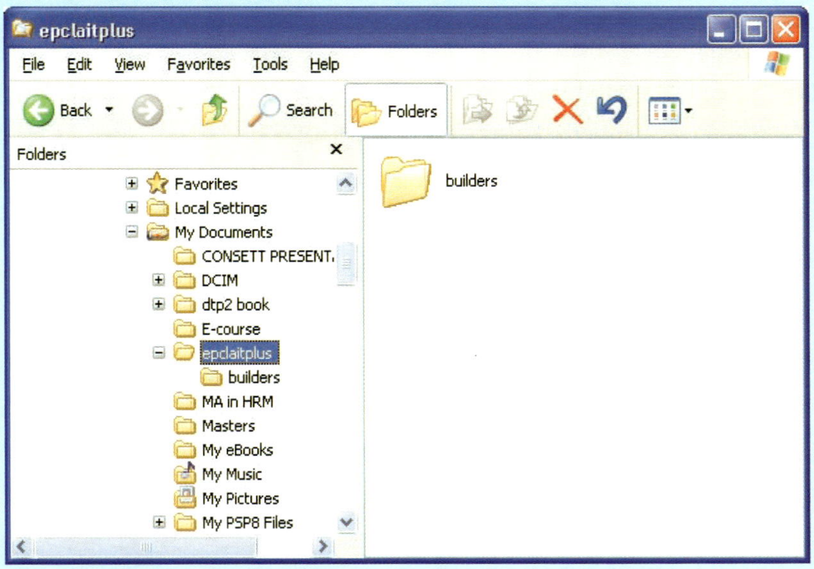

In the assessment, folders must be created as specified – and separate folders should be created unless you are specifically asked to create subfolders.

Organising files and folders

Folders are used to save related files. You can create new folders and subfolders (a folder within a folder). By organising files and folders your work should become more efficient and you will be able to locate files quickly.

- Looking at the Desktop
- Working with Windows Explorer
  - How your PC stores files and folders
  - Introducing Windows Explorer
  - Selecting files and folders
  - **Organising your files and folders**
  - **Recognising file types**
  - **Finding files and folders**
  - **Taking a snapshot of your screen**
  - **Using Microsoft Windows Help**
  - Exercise on Windows Explorer
  - Task on Windows Explorer
- Getting started with word processing
- Entering and editing text
- Changing the look of documents
- Structuring your documents
- Borders and tables
- Working with graphics and data objects
- Publishing your work

Moving a file is different from copying and if you are asked to move a file it should only be shown in one folder.

Skill Builder **1.3**

1. Launch Windows Explorer and create a new folder *build1* in your working area.
2. Create a new subfolder within the *build1* folder named *data*.
3. Move the files *text* and *image* from *My Documents* into the *data* folder.
4. Copy the files *graph* and *info* from *My Documents* into the *data* folder.
5. Capture a screen shot of the contents of the *build1* folder.
6. Paste this image into WordPad.
7. Capture a screen shot of the contents of the *data* folder.
8. Paste this image into WordPad.
9. Add your name and centre number and print, save and close the WordPad document.

Your screen shot of the data folder should look something like this

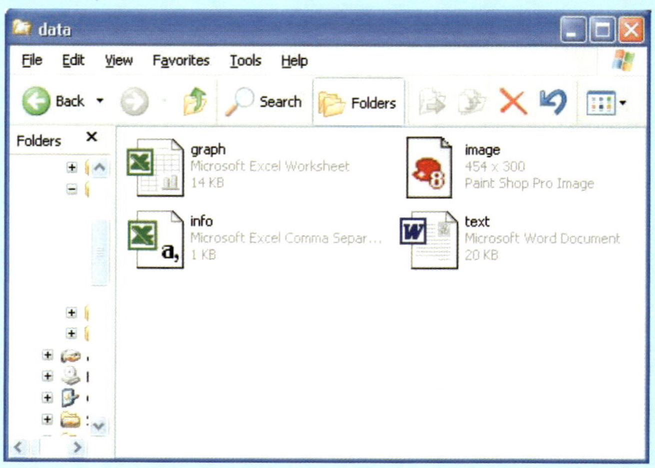

Getting started with word processing

Microsoft Word® menus and toolbars

In Word, as in all true Windows applications, all of its features can be reached through the menu system. Most are also available as buttons on the toolbars, and the ones that you will use most often are on the Standard and Formatting toolbars.

- Looking at the Desktop
- Working with Windows Explorer
- Getting started with word processing
  - **Launching Microsoft Word**
  - **Menu and toolbar basics**
  - **More about toolbars**
  - Opening and creating documents
  - Saving a document
  - Using Microsoft Office Help
  - Closing the document and application
  - Exercise on Getting started with word processing
- Entering and editing text
- Changing the look of documents
- Structuring your documents
- Borders and tables
- Working with graphics and data objects
- Publishing your work

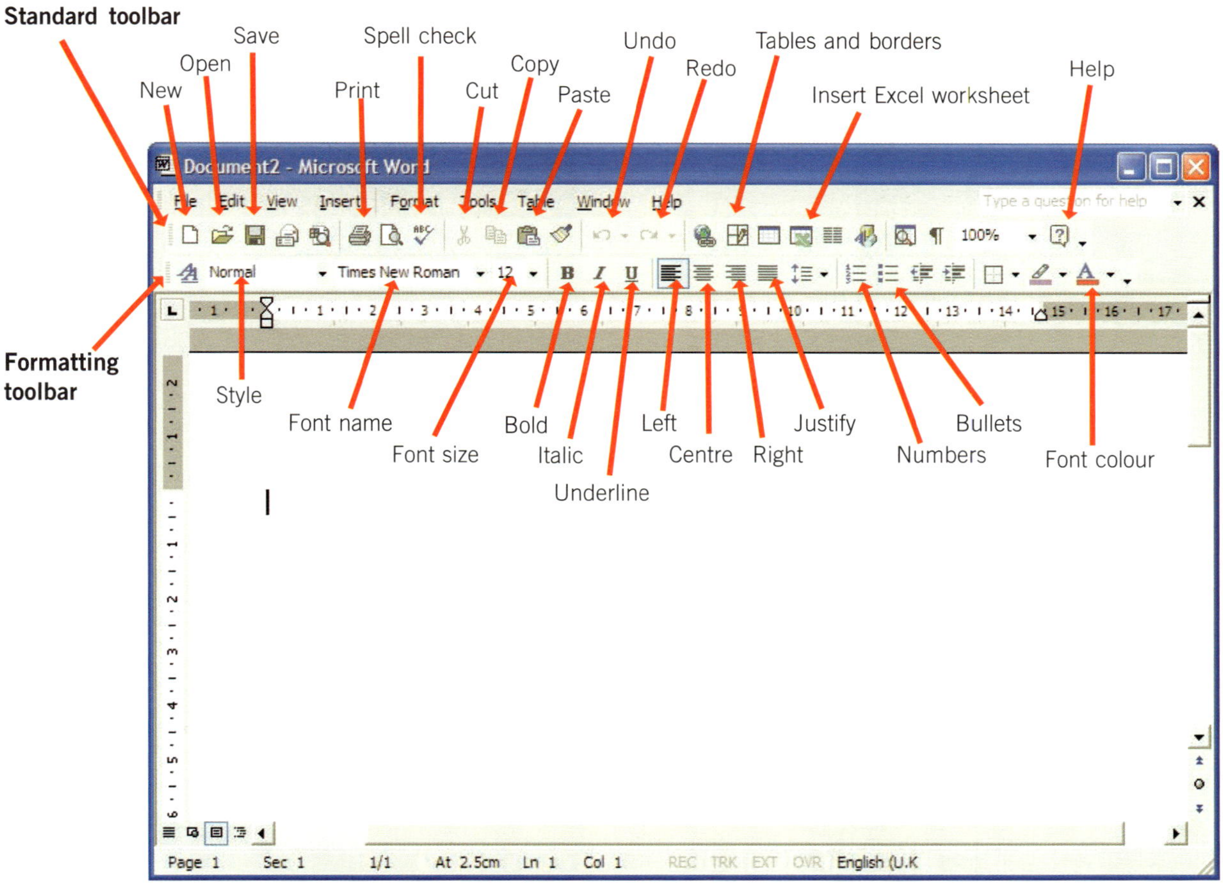

You can increase the size of toolbar icons, if required. To do this, right-click on any toolbar and select **Customize...** In the dialogue box, go to the **Options** tab and tick the **Large icons** checkbox.

Opening documents

In this section you will open a text file (one which has no formatting and can be opened in different applications) and save it as a word processing file. This allows you to apply word processing features to the document.

- Looking at the Desktop
- Working with Windows Explorer
- Getting started with word processing
  - Launching Microsoft Word
  - Menu and toolbar basics
  - More about toolbars
  - **Opening and creating documents**
  - Saving a document
  - Using Microsoft Office Help
  - Closing the document and application
  - Exercise on Getting started with word processing
- Entering and editing text
- Changing the look of documents
- Structuring your documents
- Borders and tables
- Working with graphics and data objects
- Publishing your work

If you forget to save your files in the application file type, e.g. as .doc but save them as .txt, when you re-open the file you will find that you have lost all the formatting you have applied within the document.

To find .txt files you need to display **All files** from the **Files of type:** drop-down box in Microsoft Word.

Skill Builder 1.4

1. Create a new folder in your working area and name this *Task1*.
2. Copy the file *open.txt* from the Resource Bank into your new folder *Task1*.
3. Open Microsoft Word and then open the text file *open.txt*.
4. Save the file as *open.doc* in the *Task1* folder as a Word document.

Your solution should be similar to this

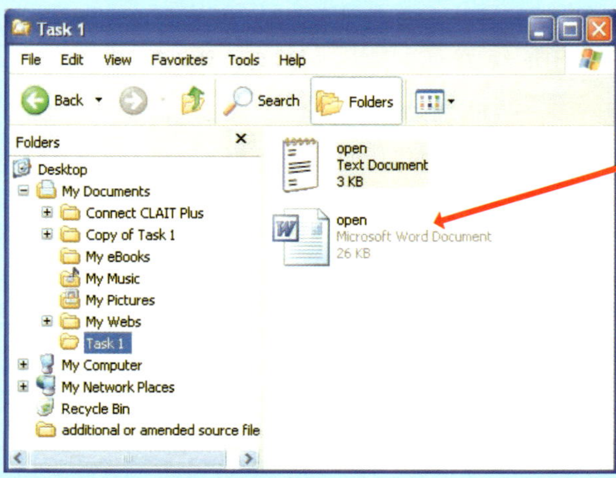

Word documents have the **W** icon and the description 'Microsoft Word Document'

Saving files

Many applications allow you to open a file in one format and save it in a different one.

- Looking at the Desktop
- Working with Windows Explorer
- Getting started with word processing
  - Launching Microsoft Word
  - Menu and toolbar basics
  - More about toolbars
  - Opening and creating documents
  - **Saving a document**
  - **Using Microsoft Office Help**
  - **Closing the document and application**
  - Exercise on Getting started with word processing
- Entering and editing text
- Changing the look of documents
- Structuring your documents
- Borders and tables
- Working with graphics and data objects
- Publishing your work

Skill Builder **1.5**

1 Create a subfolder of *Task1* and name it *text*.

2 Copy the file *blank.txt* into this folder.

3 Open the file and save this as *grammar.doc* using Microsoft Word in the folder *text*.

4 Provide a screen print to show evidence of saving this correctly.

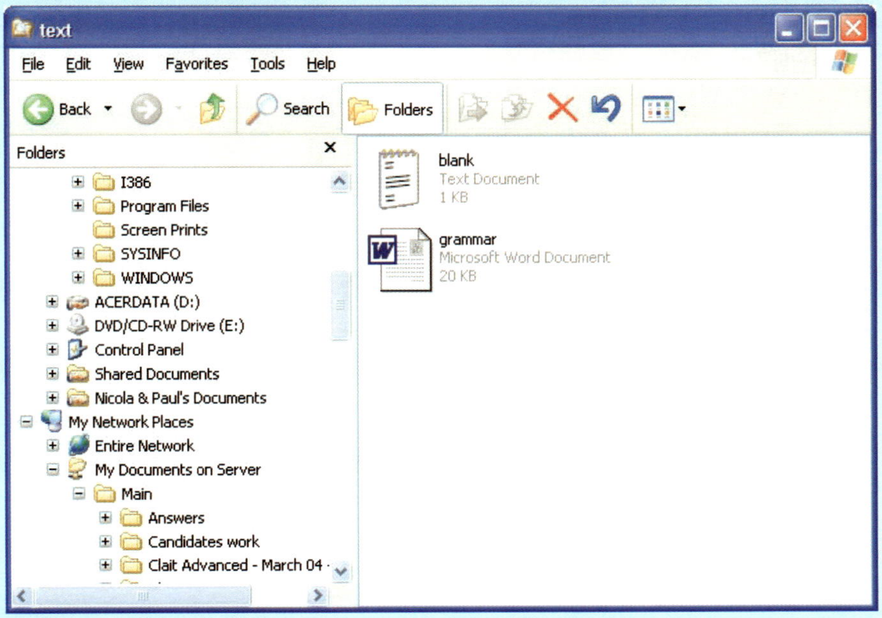

Your screen should show the *blank.txt* file in its original format and the *grammar.doc* file as a Word document.

Entering and editing text

Moving and duplicating text

You can move a word, sentence or paragraph of text from one place to another in a document or you can copy (duplicate) it. When text is copied the original text remains where it is and a copy is placed somewhere else in the document.

- Looking at the Desktop
- Working with Windows Explorer
- Getting started with word processing
- Entering and editing text
  - Inserting text
  - Useful keys on your keyboard
  - Selecting text
  - Moving and duplicating text
  - Deleting and replacing text
  - Checking spelling and grammar
  - Finding and replacing text
  - Exercise on Entering and editing text
- Changing the look of documents
- Structuring your documents
- Borders and tables
- Working with graphics and data objects
- Publishing your work

Cuts the selected text, but keeps a copy

Copies the selected text

Pastes the copied text in at the insertion point

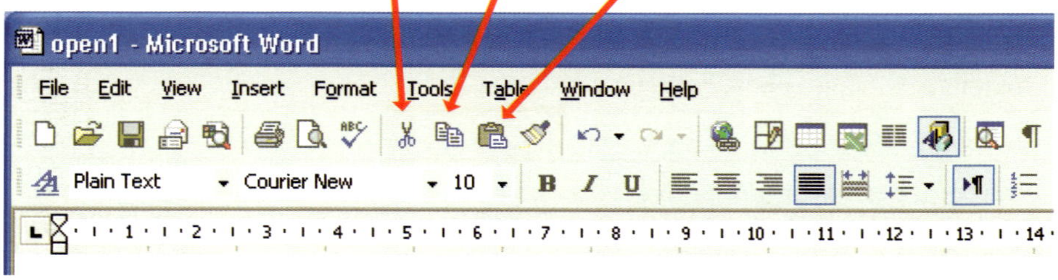

Skill Builder 1.6

1. Open Microsoft Word, and open the document file *open.doc*.
2. Highlight the subheading **Proofread** and the text beneath ending … **when you really mean "a lot"**. Click on the **Cut** icon.
3. Move the cursor to before the subheading **Tables** and click on the **Paste** icon.
4. Ensure that the spacing is consistent before and after each paragraph. Remember that you can show the paragraph marks ¶ to check this.
5. Save the document as *open1.doc*.
6. Copy the first paragraph beginning, **This text** … and ending …**a final integrated document** by clicking on the **Copy** icon. Move the cursor to the very end of the document and click on the **Paste** icon to make this new text the last paragraph of this document.

7 Save the document using the same filename (*open1.doc*) and close the file.

Your solution should be similar to that provided below:

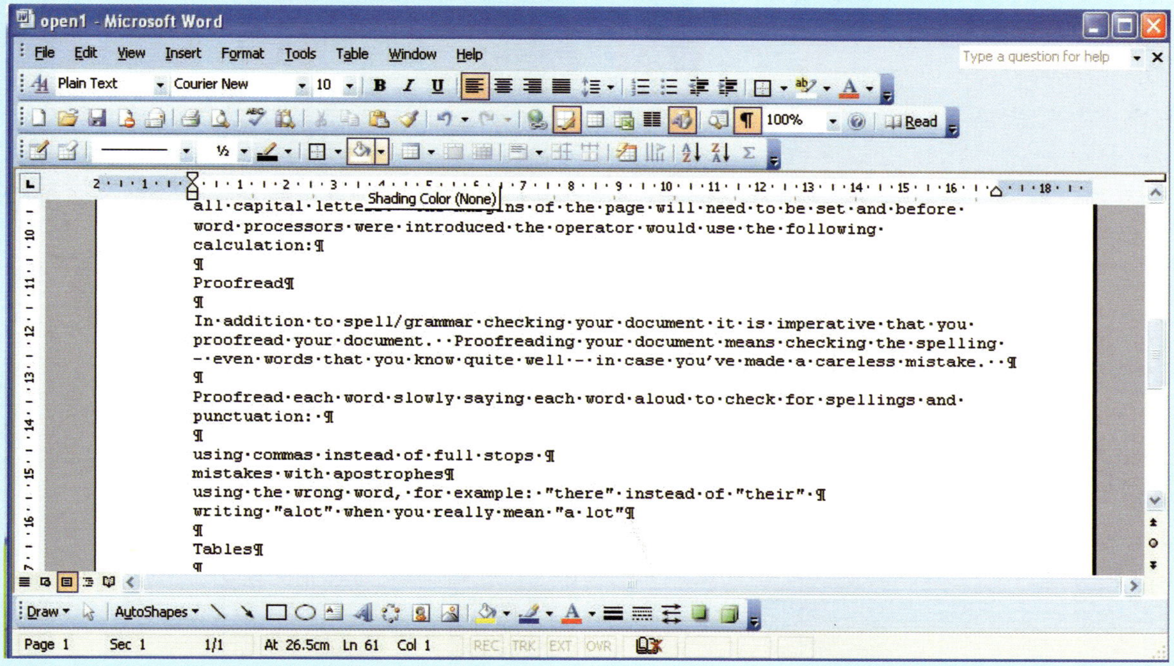

Please note: this document contains deliberate spelling mistakes which will be corrected later in the book.

Checking spelling and grammar

You should always spell check your document and proofread it carefully before it is printed. In Word it is easy to spell check a word or the whole document.

- Looking at the Desktop
- Working with Windows Explorer
- Getting started with word processing
- Entering and editing text
  - Inserting text
  - Useful keys on your keyboard
  - Selecting text
  - Moving and duplicating text
  - Deleting and replacing text
  - **Checking spelling and grammar**
  - Finding and replacing text
  - Exercise on Entering and editing text
- Changing the look of documents
- Structuring your documents
- Borders and tables
- Working with graphics and data objects
- Publishing your work

Although the software may have identified spelling errors for you, you should proofread the document, carefully checking each word against the printed text.

Skill Builder 1.7

1 Open the file *open1.doc* and spell check the entire document. Click on the **Spelling and Grammar** icon.

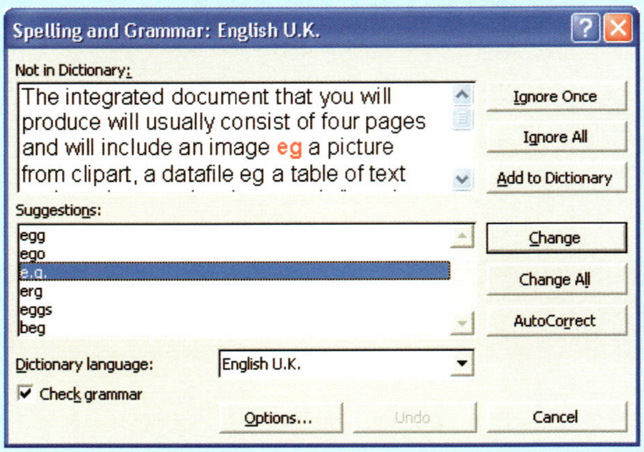

2 Save the document as *open1.doc* and close the file.

Check as you type

To check spelling and grammar as you type – open the **Tools** menu and select **Options**. Tick the boxes **Check Spelling as you type** and **Check grammar as you type** on the **Spelling and Grammar** tab.

While you are typing, you can right-click with the mouse on individual words that have a red line underneath them to spell check the word, or those with a green line underneath to check the grammar.

In the assignment, specialist words and names, e.g. Wordsworth, Shakespeare, have already been checked for spelling errors, so will not need to be checked.

Finding and replacing text

It is quick and easy in Word to find one word and replace it with another. You should do this using the feature in the software rather than manually trying to find each word in the document and then replacing it.

- Looking at the Desktop
- Working with Windows Explorer
- Getting started with word processing
- Entering and editing text
  - Inserting text
  - Useful keys on your keyboard
  - Selecting text
  - Moving and duplicating text
  - Deleting and replacing text
  - Checking spelling and grammar
  - **Finding and replacing text**
  - Exercise on Entering and editing text
- Changing the look of documents
- Structuring your documents
- Borders and tables
- Working with graphics and data objects
- Publishing your work

Skill Builder 1.8

1. Open the file *open1.doc* and search for the word information and replace it with the word data.
2. Click on the **Edit** menu and select the **Replace** option. Type information into the **Find what:** box and data in the **Replace with:** box.
3. Save the document as *open1.doc* and close the file.

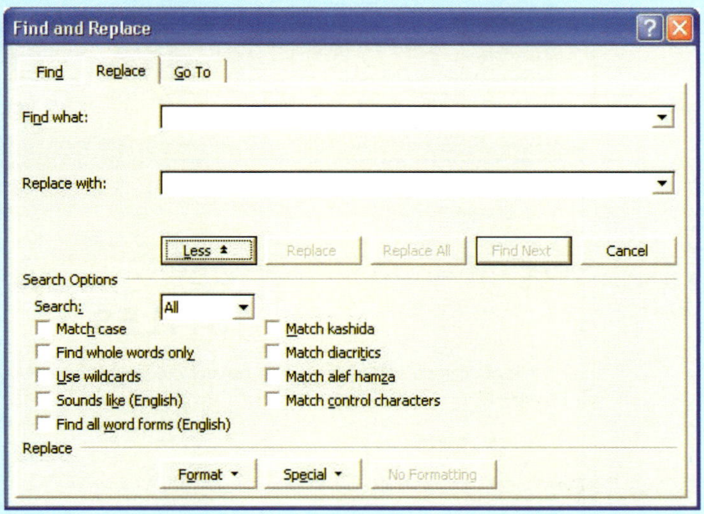

When using Find and Replace, only replace the words requested, e.g. if you are asked to search for IT and replace with Information Technology be careful that you do not replace words such as 'sit' or 'mite' which contain the letters IT. To do this, turn on the **Find whole words only** option.

Changing the look of documents

Styles and house styles

In the CLAIT Plus assessment you will be provided with a house style sheet which may be similar to that shown below.

- Looking at the Desktop
- Working with Windows Explorer
- Getting started with word processing
- Entering and editing text
- Changing the look of documents
  - What is formatting?
  - Formatting test
  - Aligning paragraphs
  - Changing line and paragraph spacing
  - Working with styles
  - Bullets and numbering
  - Using paragraphs and line breaks
  - Setting and using tabs
  - Exercise on Changing the look of documents
- Structuring your documents
- Borders and tables
- Working with graphics and data objects
- Publishing your work

Skill Builder 1.9

1 Apply this house style to the file *styles.doc*.

House Style Sheet for styles.doc

Style	Font	Font Size	Enhancement	Alignment
Heading	Sans serif	24 pt	Bold, capitals	Centre
Sub-heading	Serif	16 pt	Underline	Left
Body Text	Sans serif	12 pt	None	Left
Bullet Text	Serif	12 pt	Italics, double line spacing, bullet	Left

2 Save the file as *style1.doc*.

Your solution should look similar to this

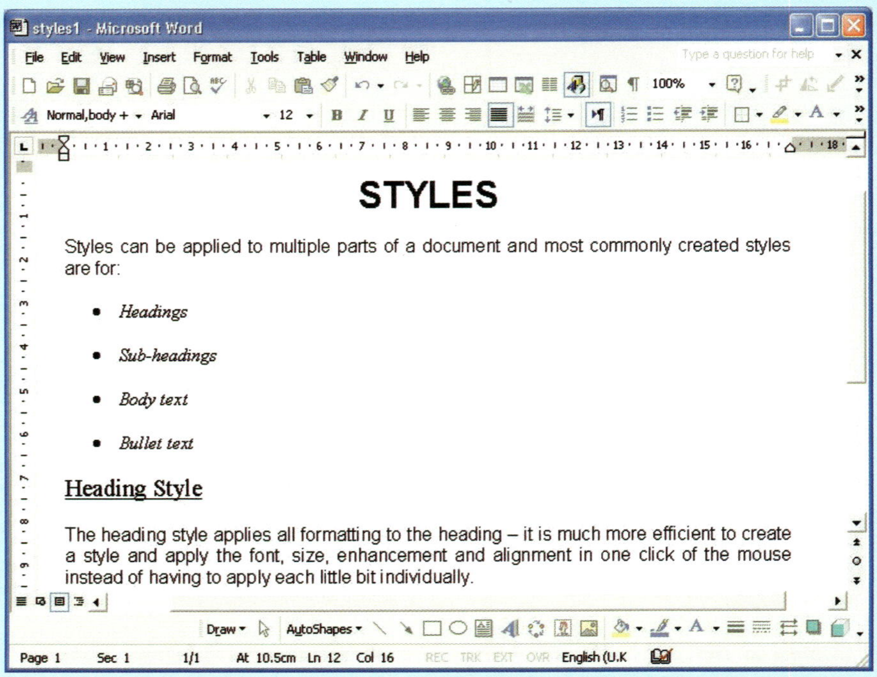

Line spacing and bullets

In the following Skill Builder you will adjust the line spacing of the text and apply bullet characters to specified text.

Any text that is changed should still show consistent blank lines (clear line spaces) above and below paragraphs.

- Looking at the Desktop
- Working with Windows Explorer
- Getting started with word processing
- Entering and editing text
- Changing the look of documents
  - What is formatting?
  - Formatting test
  - Aligning paragraphs
  - Changing line and paragraph spacing
  - Working with styles
  - **Bullets and numbering**
  - Using paragraphs and line breaks
  - Setting and using tabs
  - Exercise on Changing the look of documents
- Structuring your documents
- Borders and tables
- Working with graphics and data objects
- Publishing your work

Skill Builder **1.10**

1 In the document *open1.doc*, find the paragraph starting:
Proofread each word slowly saying each word aloud

2 Apply a bullet character to the next four short lines.

3 Change the line spacing of this bulleted text to double line spacing.

4 Save the document as *enhance.doc* and close the file.

Your screen should be similar to this

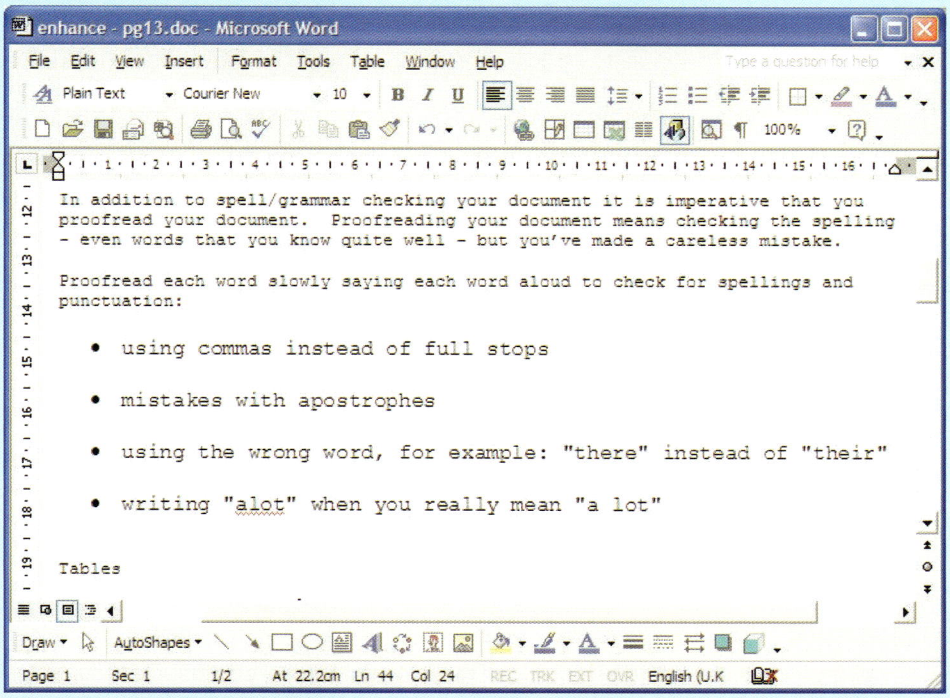

The easiest way to check for consistent line spacing is to show the non-printing characters – click ¶ to toggle them on and off.

Using paragraphs, line breaks and styles

In Word once you have filled a page full of text the software will automatically insert a page break. You can manually insert a page break to keep subheadings and text together or to insert space where an image could be placed later.

Skill Builder 1.11

1 Open the file *enhance.doc* and find the following text:

Proofread each word slowly saying each word aloud to check for spellings and punctuation:

Enter a paragraph break at the end of this paragraph to insert a clear blank line between this and the next line of text.

2 The document contains the following heading:

Unit 1 – Create, manage and integrate files

Apply a suitable serif font (e.g. Times New Roman) with bold and underline enhancement using a font size of 24 pt.

3 The document contains the following subheadings:

Integrated Document
House Style Sheet
Proofread
Tables

Create a subheading style using a suitable serif font with italics enhancement of size 16 pt. Save the style as *subhead*.

Apply this style to the subheadings listed above.

In Word 2002/2003, to create a new style, open the **Format** menu and select **Styles and Formatting...** then click the **New Style** button in the task pane.

In Word 2000, open the **Format** menu and select **Style...** then click the **New...** button in the **Style** dialogue box.

4 Create a new style named *body* for the remaining body text in the document using a sans serif font with 12 pt size and justified alignment. Apply this style to the remaining body text.

5 Save the file as *enhance.doc* and print one copy. Close the file.

Your screen should look similar to this.

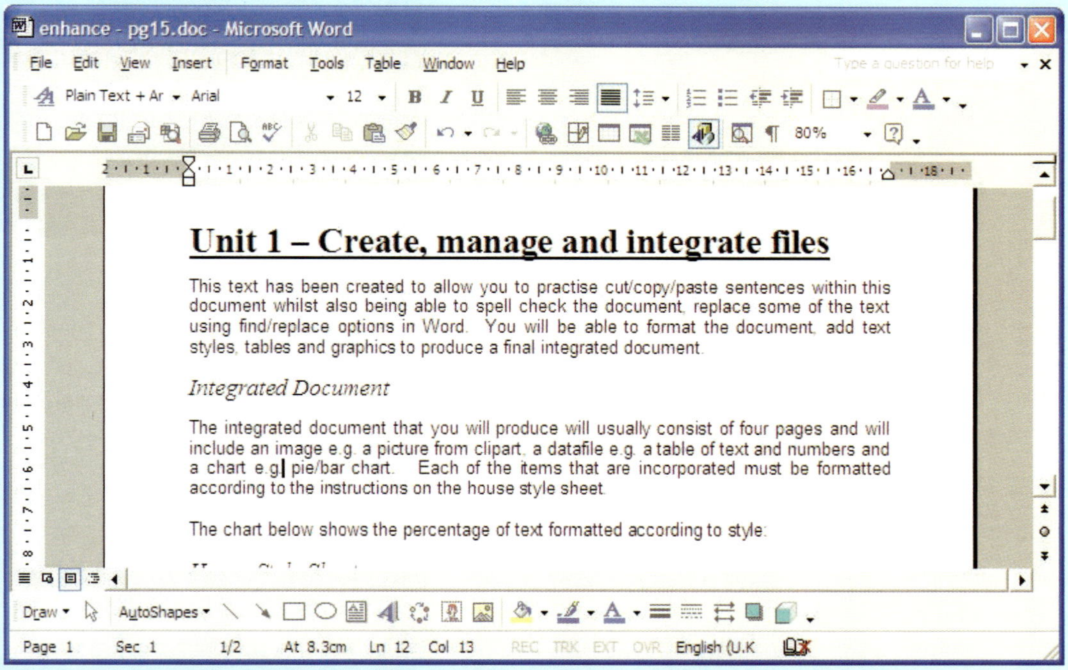

The **Format Painter** function can be used to copy the formatting from text to other text. To use it, highlight some of the formatted text. Click on the **Format Painter** icon. Highlight the text to be formatted and release the mouse button.

Symbols

You can insert special symbols or characters into text using the **Insert** menu. Word has a number of sets of symbols which can be inserted, including Latin, Greek and Special Characters.

- Looking at the Desktop
- Working with Windows Explorer
- Getting started with word processing
- Entering and editing text
- Changing the look of documents
  - What is formatting?
  - Formatting test
  - Aligning paragraphs
  - Changing line and paragraph spacing
  - Working with styles
  - Bullets and numbering
  - Using paragraphs and line breaks
  - Setting and using tabs
  - **Exercise on Changing the look of documents**
- Structuring your documents
- Borders and tables
- Working with graphics and data objects
- Publishing your work

In the assignment you will be asked to insert a symbol or special character, for example, symbols such as ½, © or • or special characters such as Ç and ë.

Skill Builder 1.12

1 Open the file *enhance.doc* and move the cursor to the next clear line at the end of the sentence: The margins of the page will need to be set and before word processors were introduced the operator would use the following calculation:

2 Create a new line space and key in the following text inserting a special symbol for the division (÷) sign:

Page size – typing width ÷ 2 = the amount to set two equal margins.

3 Save the document as *enhance.doc* and close the file.

Your document should look similar to this

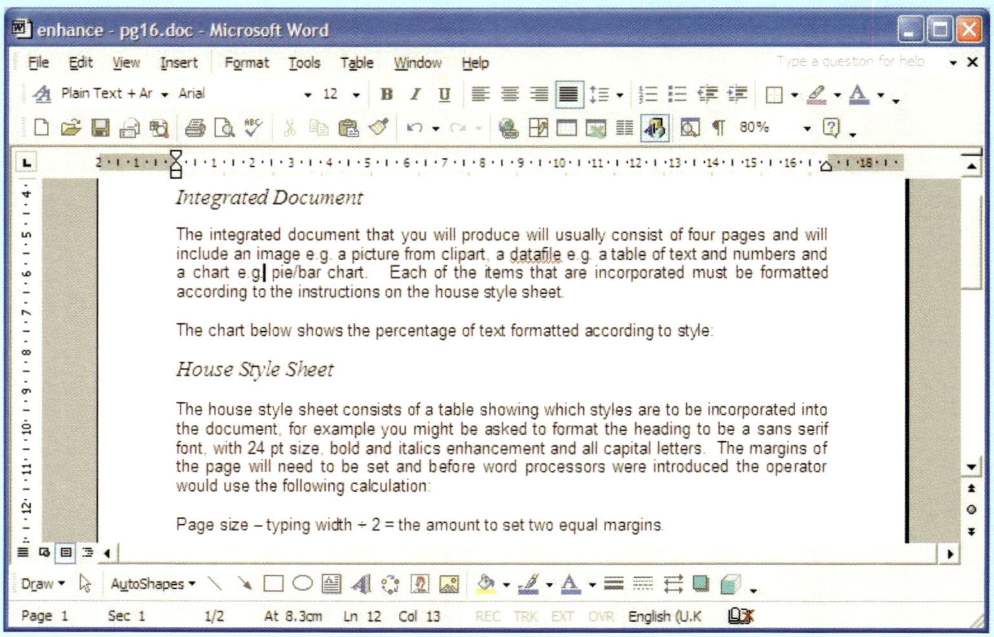

Structuring your documents

Pages and Page Setup

- Looking at the Desktop
- Working with Windows Explorer
- Getting started with word processing
- Entering and editing text
- Changing the look of documents
- Structuring your documents
  - **Headers and footers**
  - **Inserting page numbers and dates**
  - **Page breaks**
  - **Changing page setup**
  - Exercise on Structuring your documents
  - Task on Structuring your documents
- Borders and tables
- Working with graphics and data objects
- Publishing your work

Documents are usually printed on A4 paper which is the industry standard size in the UK. A4 paper can be displayed portrait (shortest edge at the top) or landscape (longest edge at the top).

A4 Portrait	A4 Landscape
210 x 297 mm	297 x 210 mm

The margins of the page allow you to change how much white space is visible between the edge of the paper and your text. Usually the margins in Word are set by default to 2.54 cm or (1 inch).

The page orientation and margins are changed through the **File > Page Setup** menu command.

Skill Builder **1.13**

1. Open the text file *open.txt* and save as *page* in your software's normal file type.
2. Select **File > Page Setup** and check that the paper size is shown as A4 portrait.
3. Change the margins to 4 cm all round (top, bottom, left and right).
4. Save the file as *page* and close the file.

Mini Assignment 1.1

You are working as the administration assistant for Alma Electronics and have been asked to amend the following document *alma.txt* as shown below and check the document carefully before it is sent to print.

1 Create a new folder named *mini* and copy the file *alma.txt* into it.

2 Open the file *alma.txt* into a word processing package and save as *mini1.doc*.

3 Make amendments to the document as shown opposite.

4 Spell check the document.

5 Search the document for the word 'Alma' and replace it with the word 'Osborne'.

6 Apply the house style to the document as shown below.

7 Key in the following text as a new paragraph before the sentence:

The price of creating...

and inserting the special symbol in the name at the start:

Chloë Jackson, one of our many satisfied customers, said that "Osborne Electronics were extremely efficient and provided a cost effective service for my daughter's wedding day".

8 Proofread the document carefully and save as *mini1.doc*.

9 Print one copy and provide to your tutor for checking.

House Style Sheet for alma.txt

- A4 Portrait
- Margins Top: 2 cm
  Bottom: 2 cm
  Left: 2 cm
  Right: 2 cm

Style	Font	Font Size	Enhancement	Alignment
Heading	Serif	24 pt	Bold, capitals	Centre
Subheading	Serif	16 pt	Italics	Left
Body Text	Sans serif	12 pt	None	Justify
Bullet Text	Serif	12 pt	Bold and 1.5 line spacing, with bullet character	Left

A sample solution is given on page 20. Use this as a guide.

alma.txt

ALMA ELECTRONICS

Heading Style

Our Company

Subheading Style

Alma Electronics are a new company who are able to provide advice and support relating to digital photography. We are a newly established business in this area and have grown rapidly over the last three years building a successful home business into a thriving small business employing 2 other members of staff. We are a family owned business and strive to provide an all round service. The following chart shows the growth in sales over the past 5 years:

Move

We are able to download your photographs from any type of media card and either save these pictures to CD or print them out to your requirements.

Photographs

Subheading Style

We print photographs using the most up-to-date digital technology using specially prepared papers with either a matt or glossy finish. The papers come in several sizes including 4x6, 7x5, A4 and A3. Photographs can also be printed out on t-shirts or imposed into other pictures to create your own design.

Moving Pictures

Subheading Style

We can capture pictures from your camcorder and save these in various formats, such as:

VideoCD
Mpeg1
Mpeg2

Bullet style

which can then be played in most conventional DVD players.

Insert the text from step 7 here as a new paragraph.

The price of creating moving pictures is shown below:

OSBORNE ELECTRONICS

Our Company

Osborne Electronics are a new company who are able to provide advice and support relating to digital photography. We are a newly established business in this area and have grown rapidly over the last three years building a successful home business into a thriving small business employing 2 other members of staff. We are a family owned business and strive to provide an all round service. The following chart shows the growth in sales over the past 5 years:

Photographs

We are able to download your photographs from any type of media card and either save these pictures to CD or print them out to your requirements.

We print photographs using the most up-to-date digital technology using specially prepared papers with either a matt or glossy finish. The papers come in several sizes including 4x6, 7x5, A4 and A3. Photographs can also be printed out on t-shirts or imposed into other pictures to create your own design.

Moving Pictures

We can capture pictures from your camcorder and save these in various formats, such as:

- **VideoCD**
- **Mpeg1**
- **Mpeg2**

which can then be played in most conventional DVD players.

Chloë Jackson, one of our many satisfied customers, said that "Osborne Electronics were extremely efficient and provided a cost effective service for my daughter's wedding day".

The price of creating moving pictures is shown below:

Borders and tables

Creating tables

In the CLAIT Plus assessment you will be required to key in a table from record cards, where you select some but not all of the information to be input.

- Looking at the Desktop
- Working with Windows Explorer
- Getting started with word processing
- Entering and editing text
- Changing the look of documents
- Structuring your documents
- Borders and tables
  - **Borders and shading**
  - **Creating tables**
  - Rearranging tables
  - Changing the look of tables
  - Exercise on Borders and tables
  - Task on Borders and tables
- Working with graphics and data objects
- Publishing your work

Skill Builder **1.14**

1. Open a new Word document and create a 5-column table using the column headings *Feature*, *Font*, *Pt Size*, *Alignment* and *To be Used*. Take your data from the record cards shown here, key in only that data where the record shows 'Y' in the *To be Used* cell.
2. Ensure that the data is shown in full and no words are split incorrectly in the table.
3. Save the file as *table1.doc*, print one copy and close the file.

Feature	Heading		
Font	Arial	Pt Size	36
Enhancement	Bold	Alignment	Centre
Style Name	Headline	To be Used	Y
Description	The main heading of the document		

Feature	Heading2		
Font	Arial	Pt Size	30
Enhancement	Italic	Alignment	Left
Style Name	Chapter heading	To be Used	N
Description	Style to be set for chapter headings within the document		

Feature	Subheadings		
Font	Times New Roman	Pt Size	16
Enhancement	Underline	Alignment	Right
Style Name	Subhead	To be Used	Y
Description	To be used for all subheadings within the document		

Feature	Body Text		
Font	Comic Sans MS	Pt Size	12
Enhancement	None	Alignment	Justified
Style Name	Body	To be Used	Y
Description	To be used for most of the text in the document		

Feature	Bullet Text		
Font	Georgia	Pt Size	14
Enhancement	Italics	Alignment	Centre
Style Name	Bullet	To be Used	Y
Description	To be applied to bullet text only		

Feature	Header		
Font	Verdana	Pt Size	10
Enhancement	None	Alignment	Left
Style Name	Header	To be Used	N
Description	To be applied to text in the header space only		

Feature	Plain Text		
Font	Courier New	Pt Size	10
Enhancement	None	Alignment	Right
Style Name	Text	To be Used	N
Description	To be applied to plain text only		

Your solution should be similar to this

Feature	Font	Pt Size	Alignment	To be Used
Heading	Arial	36	Centre	Y
Subheadings	Times New Roman	16	Right	Y
Body Text	Comic Sans MS	12	Justified	Y
Bullet Text	Georgia	14	Centre	Y

Rearranging tables

In Word you can rearrange tables by moving columns or rows. You can select a whole column or row and cut and paste it to a new location.

- Looking at the Desktop
- Working with Windows Explorer
- Getting started with word processing
- Entering and editing text
- Changing the look of documents
- Structuring your documents
- Borders and tables
  - Borders and shading
  - Creating tables
  - **Rearranging tables**
  - Changing the look of tables
  - Exercise on Borders and tables
  - Task on Borders and tables
- Working with graphics and data objects
- Publishing your work

Skill Builder **1.15**

1 Open the file *table1.doc* ensuring that all data in the table is still shown in full.

2 Move the *Alignment* column so that it becomes the second column in the table following the *Feature* column.

3 Ensure that the data is still shown in full and words have not been split.

4 Save the file as *table1.doc* and keep open for the next Skill Builder.

Your solution should be similar to this

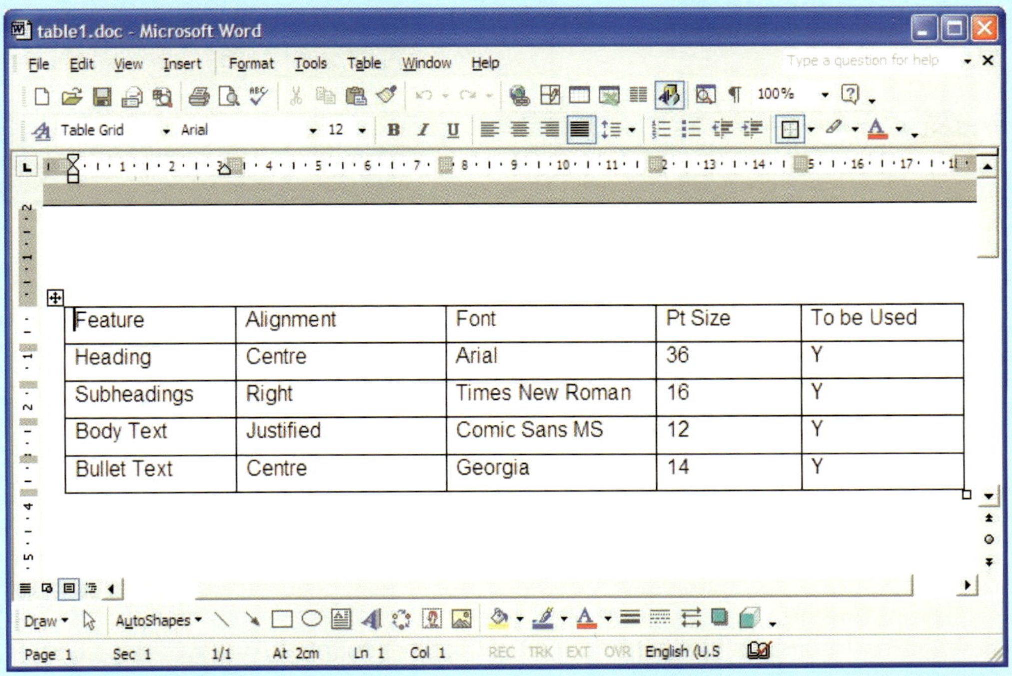

Feature	Alignment	Font	Pt Size	To be Used
Heading	Centre	Arial	36	Y
Subheadings	Right	Times New Roman	16	Y
Body Text	Justified	Comic Sans MS	12	Y
Bullet Text	Centre	Georgia	14	Y

Changing the look of tables

In the following Skill Builder you will use the table that you have created above but you will now change the alignment of the data within the columns. You will notice that the text in the table is all currently left aligned.

- Looking at the Desktop
- Working with Windows Explorer
- Getting started with word processing
- Entering and editing text
- Changing the look of documents
- Structuring your documents
- Borders and tables
  - Borders and shading
  - Creating tables
  - Rearranging tables
  - Changing the look of tables
  - Exercise on Borders and tables
  - Task on Borders and tables
- Working with graphics and data objects
- Publishing your work

Skill Builder 1.16

1 Open the file *table1.doc* and change the alignment of the columns as follows:

Column	Alignment
Feature	centre
Alignment	right
Font	left
Pt Size	centre
To be used	centre

2 Save the file as *table1.doc* and close the file.

Any time that you are unsure of how to work through a Skill Builder, refer back to the 'Working with graphics and data objects' section on the e-course.

Borders and tables

In Word you can add borders, border art or shading to your table. Borders can be added on the outside or as gridlines. Cells can be shaded and you can even reverse the colouring so that cells are shaded black with white text.

- Looking at the Desktop
- Working with Windows Explorer
- Getting started with word processing
- Entering and editing text
- Changing the look of documents
- Structuring your documents
- Borders and tables
  - Borders and shading
  - Creating tables
  - Rearranging tables
  - Changing the look of tables
  - Exercise on Borders and tables
  - Task on Borders and tables
- Working with graphics and data objects
- Publishing your work

Skill Builder 1.17

1 Open the file *table1.doc*.

2 Change the page orientation to landscape with 2 cm margins all round (top, bottom, left, right).

3 Insert a header: Your name and today's date.

4 Change the column headings to bold with centre alignment.

5 Change the column headings to be italics.

6 Apply gridlines to the table if these have not automatically been applied.

7 Shade the column headings with a 45% grey fill effect.

8 Save the file as *table2.doc*, print one copy of the file and close the file.

Your solution should be similar to this

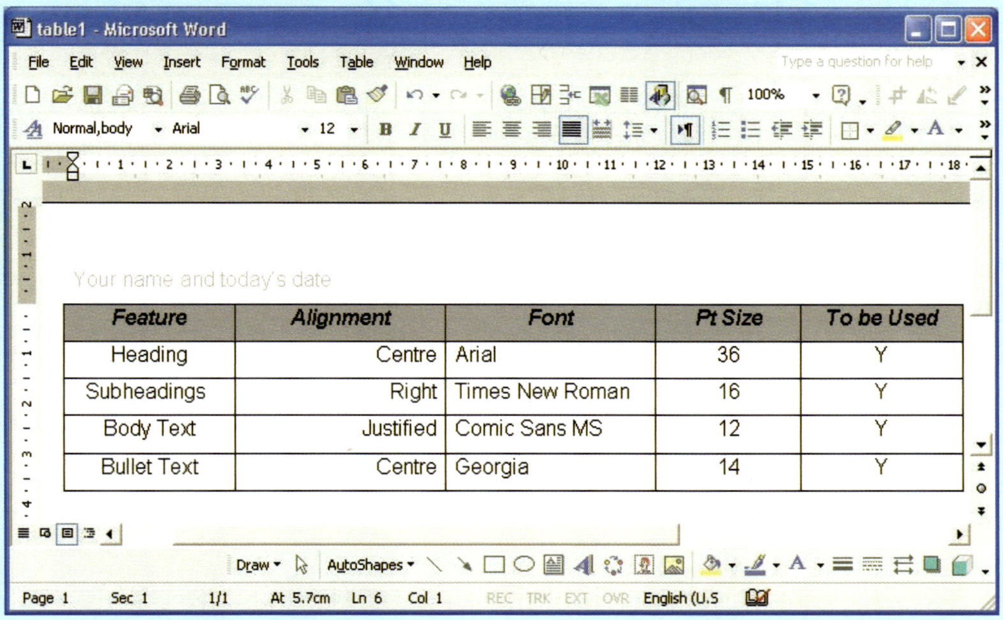

Feature	*Alignment*	*Font*	*Pt Size*	*To be Used*
Heading	Centre	Arial	36	Y
Subheadings	Right	Times New Roman	16	Y
Body Text	Justified	Comic Sans MS	12	Y
Bullet Text	Centre	Georgia	14	Y

Working with graphics and data objects

Modifying graphics

You can change the size of Clip Art images or photographs that you import into your document. You can also change the colours, contrast and brightness.

- Looking at the Desktop
- Working with Windows Explorer
- Getting started with word processing
- Entering and editing text
- Changing the look of documents
- Structuring your documents
- Borders and tables
- Working with graphics and data objects
  - Adding existing graphics
  - Modifying graphics
  - Copying data from other applications
  - Changing the look of an imported chart
  - Exercise on Working with graphics and data objects
  - Task on Working with graphics and data objects
- Publishing your work

Skill Builder **1.18**

1. Open the document *enhance.doc*. Insert a clear line space after the heading.
2. Insert a suitable Clip Art image centred underneath the heading.
3. Resize the image so that it is approximately 3 cm by 3 cm.
4. Open the document *table2.doc* and copy the table into *enhance.doc*. Insert the following text before the Proofread paragraph, then place the table below it.
   The table below shows an extract from the house style sheet:
5. Ensure that the table is still formatted correctly and the text is shown in full and none of the words are split.
6. Open Excel and locate the file *chart.xls*. Highlight the chart worksheet and copy the chart from Excel, pasting it in after the text:
   The chart below shows the percentage of text formatted according to style:
7. Apply a border to this chart.
8. Close the pie chart in Microsoft Excel and open the file *data.csv*.
9. Insert the datafile after the text:
   Percentage of errors identified by administrative team leader:
10. Format the datafile with a serif font at 16 pt size. Do not apply any gridlines or shading to this table.
11. Save the file as *integrate.doc* and then close it.

Publishing your work

Printing documents

Once you have completed your document you will need to print it out.

- Looking at the Desktop
- Working with Windows Explorer
- Getting started with word processing
- Entering and editing text
- Changing the look of documents
- Structuring your documents
- Borders and tables
- Working with graphics and data objects
- Publishing your work
  - **Previewing documents**
  - **Printing documents**
  - Exercise on Publishing your work

Skill Builder **1.19**

1 Open the *integrate.doc* file if this is not already open.

2 Proofread the document carefully, checking spelling. Check the layout of your document to ensure that spacing before and after each paragraph is consistent. You can do this by toggling on the **Show/Hide ¶** icon on the **Standard** toolbar.

3 Preview your document to check for any widows/orphans (one line of text on its own at either the bottom or top of a page).

4 Print one copy of the document. Again, proofread the document carefully checking each of the instructions against the printout.

5 Make any amendments to the document and print one final copy for checking by your tutor.

Your solution should be similar to that shown on the next three pages.

Should any of the data be changed during the assignment, e.g. if you accessed the chart data and accidentally changed 25 to 35 so that the pie charts segments are shown differently, this will incur a critical error.

Unit 1 – Create, manage and integrate files

This text has been created to allow you to practise cut/copy/paste sentences within this document whilst also being able to spell check the document, replace some of the text using find/replace options in Word. You will be able to format the document, add text styles, tables and graphics to produce a final integrated document.

Integrated Document

The integrated document that you will produce will usually consist of four pages and will include an image e.g. a picture from clipart, a datafile e.g. a table of text and numbers and a chart e.g. pie/bar chart. Each of the items that are incorporated must be formatted according to the instructions on the house style sheet.

The chart below shows the percentage of text formatted according to style:

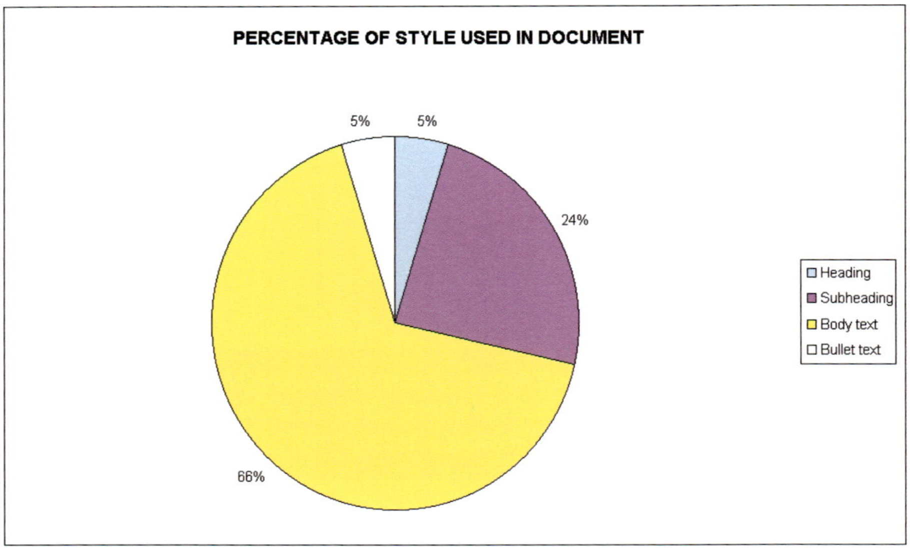

House Style Sheet

The house style sheet consists of a table showing which styles are to be incorporated into the document, for example you might be asked to format the heading to be a sans serif font, with 24 pt size, bold and italics enhancement and all capital letters. The margins of the page will need to be set and before word processors were introduced the operator would use the following calculation:

Page size – typing width ÷ 2 = the amount to set two equal margins.

The table below shows an extract from the house style sheet:

Feature	***Alignment***	***Font***	***Pt Size***	***To be used***
Heading	Centre	Arial	36	Y
Subheadings	Right	Times New Roman	16	Y
Body Text	Justified	Comic Sans MS	12	Y
Bullet Text	Centre	Georgia	14	Y

Proofread

In addition to spell/grammar checking your document it is imperative that you proofread your document. Proofreading your document means checking the spelling - even words that you know quite well - in case you've made a careless mistake.

Proofread each word slowly saying each word aloud to check for spellings and punctuation:

- using commas instead of full stops
- mistakes with apostrophes
- using the wrong word, for example: "there" instead of "their"
- writing "alot" when you really mean "a lot"

Tables

You will create a table from data record cards and these are provided at the end of the assignment – you will need to select relevant data from the record cards, e.g. you will only key data into the table where the start date shown on the record cards is the same as the 1 October. You will format data in the table again using the house style sheet and will include the font type, font size, enhancements and alignment of the columns of data, e.g. right align all of the dates in this table. You will probably also be asked to add borders/ shading to the table to enhance the appearance within the document.

Percentage of errors identified by administrative team leader:

Errors in a document	
Spelling	8%
Commas	4%
Apostrophes	8%
Typographical	26%
Grammatical	35%
Tense	19%

This text has been created to allow you to practise cut/copy/paste sentences within this document whilst also being able to spell check the document, replace some of the text using find/replace options in Word. You will be able to format the document, add text styles, tables and graphics to produce a final integrated document.

Mini Assignment 1.2

1. Open the file *mini1.doc* and make the changes shown on the text below.
2. Apply the formatting as listed on the house style sheet overleaf.
3. Save the file as *mini1.doc* and print out one copy for your tutor.
4. Close the file.

OSBORNE ELECTRONICS

Insert the company logo here. Centre between the margins

Our Company

Osborne Electronics are a new company who are able to provide advice and support relating to digital photography. We are a newly established business in this area and have grown rapidly over the last three years building a successful home business into a thriving small business employing 2 other members of staff. We are a family owned business and strive to provide an all round service. The following chart shows the growth in sales over the past 5 years:

Insert the chart growth here. Centre between the margins

Photographs

We are able to download your photographs from any type of media card and either save these pictures to CD or print them out to your requirements.

We print photographs using the most up-to-date digital technology using specially prepared papers with either a matt or glossy finish. The papers come in several sizes including 4x6, 7x5, A4 and A3. [New Para] Photographs can also be printed out on t-shirts or imposed into other pictures to create your own design.

Insert a four-column table here extracting the data from the digital record cards, using the column headings, Size, Availability, Description, and Cost. Only include those records where the availability is October 2004. Apply an outside border only to this chart.

Moving Pictures

We can capture pictures from your camcorder and save these in various formats, such as:

- VideoCD
- Mpeg1
- Mpeg2

which can then be played in most conventional DVD players.

Chloë Jackson, one of our many satisfied customers, said that "Osborne Electronics were extremely efficient and provided a cost effective service for my daughter's wedding day".

The price of creating moving pictures is shown below:

Insert the datafile prices here. Add an outside border only to frame the data

House Style Sheet

A4 portrait

All margins:	2 cm		
Header:	Your name, today's date		
Footer:	Automatic filename (left aligned) and page number (right aligned)		
Style	**Font**	**Font Size**	**Enhancement and alignment**
Table (outside border only)	Serif	12 pt	**Column Headings:** Bold and centre **Size** – left aligned **Availability** – right aligned **Description** – left aligned **Cost** – centre
Datafile (outside border only)	Serif	12 pt	**Column Headings:** Bold and left **1st Column** – left aligned **Other columns** – centre
Chart	Apply a border to frame the chart		

Digital Record Cards

Item Photograph1	Size 4" x 5.3"	Cost £0.14	Availability October 2004
Description	Digitally enhanced photographs with edge-to-edge printing		

Item Mug	Size S, M, L	Cost £4.50	Availability November 2004
Description	Photograph applied to a plain white mug – you can add your own message		

Item Photograph2	Size 5" x 6.6"	Cost £0.19	Availability October 2004
Description	Glossy finishing removing any red eye		

Item Mouse Mat	Size One Size	Cost £6.99	Availability November 2004
Description	A photograph embedded into a coloured mouse mat of your choice		

Item Photograph3	Size 6" x 8"	Cost £0.50	Availability October 2004
Description	Larger prints with or without border		

Item T-Shirt	Size S, M, L	Cost £9.99	Availability November 2004
Description	A photograph printed onto a plain white t-shirt		

Item Photograph4	Size 8" x 10.6"	Cost £1.20	Availability October 2004
Description	Matt finish prints with optional coloured mount		

Item Photograph5	Size 12" x 16"	Cost £4.99	Availability October 2004
Description	Glossy finished digitally enhanced prints in photo album		

Units 2, 9, 10

SPREADSHEETS

A spreadsheet allows you to calculate numeric information, e.g. wages, accounts or budgeting by using simple and more advanced formulas.

Spreadsheets can produce graphical data (e.g. a pie chart) from numeric data allowing data to be more easily interpreted.

They allow you to calculate information and use projections which can assist with business planning.

Microsoft Excel® has useful functions and wizards that help you to construct formulas or produce graphs or charts by following simple steps.

- Create, manage and integrate files
- Spreadsheets
- Databases
- Presentation graphics
- E-communications

Throughout this unit you will be asked to open files that are supplied in the Resource Bank. They can be found on the Resource Bank CD or in the folder which your tutor may have set up for use with this course.

Basic concepts

Revision

Excel can be opened by double-clicking the icon on the desktop or by accessing the program from the Start menu.

The screen shot below shows the most commonly used buttons on the Standard and Formatting toolbars.

- Basic concepts
  - Launching Microsoft Excel
  - Menu and toolbar basics
  - More about toolbars
  - Creating a workbook
  - Opening a workbook
  - Saving a workbook
  - Using Microsoft Office Help
  - Closing the workbook and application
  - Exercise on Basic concepts
- Entering and formatting data
- Basic formulas and functions
- Entering and organising data
- Charts
- Customising worksheets
- Advanced formulas and functions
- Distributing your worksheets

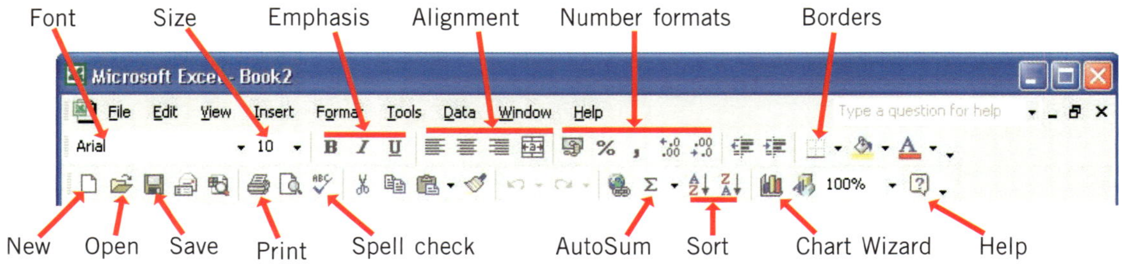

Skill Builder 2.1

1. Open Excel.
2. Open the spreadsheet file *child.xls* and save it as *child2.xls*.
3. Use the Office Assistant to get Help on formatting text.
4. Produce a screen print to show that you have accessed the correct Help page.

Your solution should be similar to this

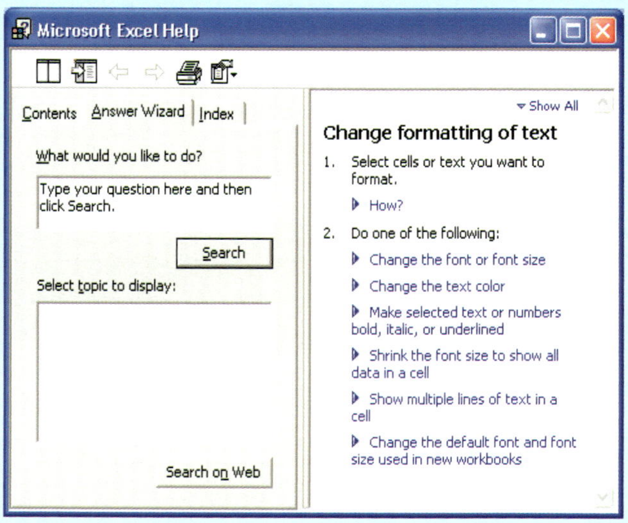

Entering and formatting data

Creating a workbook

The following Skill Builder allows you to practise creating your own workbook. Remember to key in all data as shown in the exercise and proofread carefully.

- Basic concepts
- Entering and formatting data
  - Selecting cells and ranges
  - Moving around a worksheet
  - Adding data to cells
  - Adding numbers to cells
  - Features that speed up data entry
  - Basic formatting
  - Advanced formatting
  - Formatting numbers
  - Importing text files
  - Exercise on Entering and formatting data
  - Task on Entering and formatting data
- Basic formulas and functions
- Entering and organising data
- Charts
- Customising worksheets
- Advanced formulas and functions
- Distributing your worksheets

Skill Builder 2.2

1 Open Microsoft Excel and key in the data as shown below:

Virtual Courses								
Details							Costs	
Course Title	Learner	Tutor	Course Type	Hub	Start Date	End Date	Cost	Tutor Fee
IT for beginners	Ian Newlove	Joe Smith	IT	Barnard Castle Learning Hub	21/02/2004	01/04/2004	£24.99	£6.25
Marketing	Alison Smith	Stacie Tindale	BM	Newcastle Learning Hub	26/02/2004	06/04/2004	£37.49	£9.37
Customer Care	Karen Firth	Joe Smith	BM	Barnard Castle Learning Hub	01/03/2004	10/04/2004	£16.25	£4.06
Interviewing Skills	Jean Tweddle	David Simpson	BM	Carlise Learning Hub	26/05/2004	05/07/2004	£17.49	£4.37
Coaching	Daniel West	Andrew White	BM	Bishopton Learning Hub	28/02/2004	08/04/2004	£29.99	£7.50
Intro to HTML	Amanda Russell	Susan Clements	IT	Derby Learning Hub	03/03/2004	12/04/2004	£16.25	£4.06
Creating Web Pages	Steve Richardson	Andrew White	IT	Bishopton Learning Hub	08/03/2004	17/04/2004	£9.99	£2.50
Animating Text	Janet Nolan	Claire Allerton	IT	Nottingham Learning Hub	01/03/2004	10/04/2004	£22.99	£5.75
Databases	Carolyne Elliott	Sam Lusty	IT	Somerset Learning Hub	05/03/2004	14/04/2004	£16.75	£4.19
Spreadsheets	Birhan Fioir	Alan Barwick	IT	Peterborough Learning Hub	01/03/2004	10/04/2004	£36.00	£9.00

continued...

Course Title	Learner	Tutor	Course Type	Hub	Start Date	End Date	Cost	Tutor Fee
Formulas in Excel	Ken Kenber	Andrew White	IT	Bishopton Learning Hub	01/04/2004	11/05/2004	£23.00	£5.75
Developing Yourself	Mark Hindmarsh	Andrew White	BM	Bishopton Learning Hub	31/05/2004	10/07/2004	£15.00	£3.75
Mailmerge	Nigel Brown	Kylie Broadhead	IT	Darlington Learning Hub	05/06/2004	15/07/2004	£0.00	£0.00
Intermediate IT	Helen Glover	Colin Cross	IT	Bishopton Learning Hub	28/02/2004	08/04/2004	£11.25	£2.81
Marketing	Claire Healey	Ian Woodward	BM	Barnard Castle Learning Hub	01/04/2004	11/05/2004	£15.00	£3.75
Time Management	Susan Young	Joe Smith	BM	Barnard Castle Learning Hub	02/03/2004	11/04/2004	£7.50	£1.88
Absence Management	Rosanne Clark	Steven Evans	BM	Carlise Learning Hub	01/04/2004	11/05/2004	£7.50	£1.88
Project Management	Ann Edmonds	Mary Hall	BM	Bishopton Learning Hub	15/03/2004	24/04/2004	£23.75	£5.94

2 Add two new column headings, *Balance* and *Increase* after *Tutor Fee*.

3 Key in the following data in cells O3 to P6:

Increase	7.5%
VAT	17.5%
IT Funding	£650.00
BM Funding	£825.00

4 Key in the following data in cells A27 to A33:

MANAGEMENT DATA
Total Balance
Average Balance
Max Balance
Number of IT courses
Number of BM courses

5 Save the file as *courses.xls*.

Any numeric data that is keyed incorrectly which could be used in a formula is penalised as a critical error.

Advanced formatting

As with the other units in CLAIT Plus you will be required to format the spreadsheet using a house style sheet. The house style sheet states which fonts, font sizes, enhancements and alignments are to be used.

- Basic concepts
- Entering and formatting data
  - Selecting cells and ranges
  - Moving around a worksheet
  - Adding data to cells
  - Adding numbers to cells
  - **Features that speed up data entry**
  - **Basic formatting**
  - **Advanced formatting**
  - Formatting numbers
  - Importing text files
  - Exercise on Entering and formatting data
  - Task on Entering and formatting data
- Basic formulas and functions
- Entering and organising data
- Charts
- Customising worksheets
- Advanced formulas and functions
- Distributing your worksheets

Skill Builder **2.3**

1. Open the file *nursery.csv.*
2. Change the heading 'Apple Tree Nursery' to a serif font e.g. (Times New Roman) with a point size of 24. Merge and centre the cells across the columns A–M.
3. Format the second row of headings with a sans serif font, point size 12, bold enhancement and rotated by 45^0 (*Details*, *Invoicing* and *Fee Structure*) Merge and centre *Details* across columns A-H, *Invoicing* across columns I–J, *Fee Structure* across columns L–M.
4. Apply a sans serif font, point size 12, with italics for the remaining column headings. Wrap onto two rows with top vertical alignment.
5. Ensure that the body text uses a sans serif font with point size of 10. Format all monetary amounts to two decimal places with right alignment.
6. Save the file as *nursery.xls* and close the file.

Mini Assignment 2.1

1 Using the file *courses.xls* apply the house style as listed below on the house style sheet.

House Style Sheet

Feature	**Font**	**Font size**	**Style**	**Alignment**
Main title	Serif	14 pt	Bold, framed by a border	Centered across all columns that contain data
Section headings	Serif	12 pt	Bold	Centered across the columns making up the section
Column headings	Sans serif	10 pt	Italic	Horizontal: left for column(s) of text, right for column(s) of numbers /currency unless otherwise stated. Vertical: Centre Rotated 90°
All other text	Sans serif	10 pt	–	Left unless otherwise stated
Monetary amounts	Sans serif	10 pt	2 decimal places unless specified. Not displaying the £ sign unless specified.	Right
Dates	Sans serif	10 pt	UK date format (i.e. day, month, year)	Right
Other numbers	Sans serif	10 pt	0 decimal places (unless specified)	Right

2 Save the file as *courses.xls* and close it.

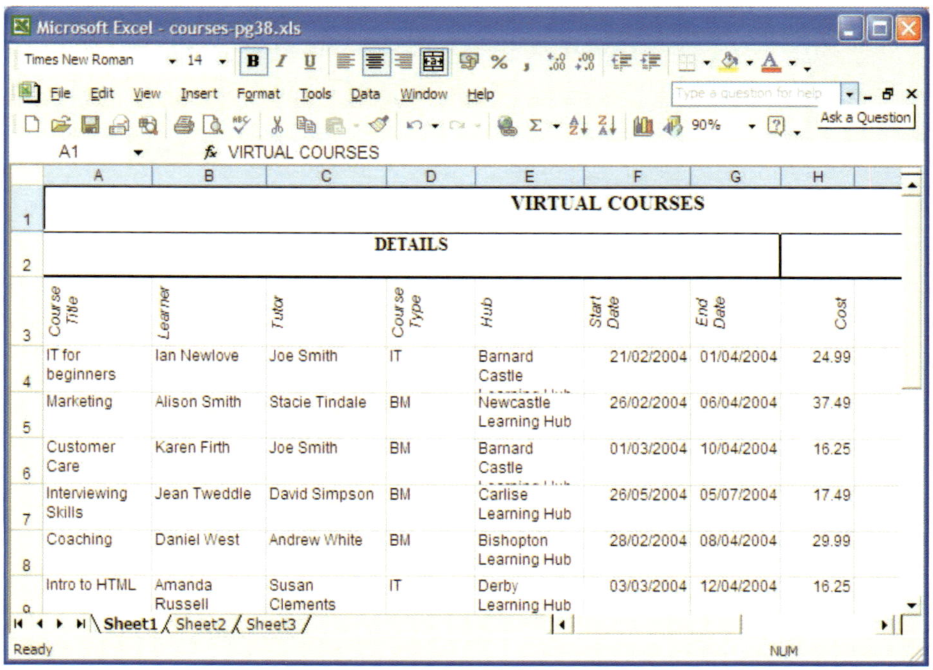

Basic formulas and functions

Entering simple formulas

You will enter simple formulas to calculate the total daily fee by adding the daily fee and the early drop off fee.

- Basic concepts
- Entering and formatting data
- Basic formulas and functions
  - Introducing simple formulas
  - Entering simple formulas
  - Combining operators in formulas
  - Using basic functions
  - Dealing with common errors in formulas
  - Using the Function Wizard
  - Exercise on Basic formulas and functions
- Entering and organising data
- Charts
- Customising worksheets
- Advanced formulas and functions
- Distributing your worksheets

Skill Builder **2.4**

1 Using the spreadsheet file *nursery.xls* calculate the *Total Daily Fee* by adding the *Daily Fee* and *Early Drop Off fee* together. Replicate this across all the records.

2 Save the file as *nursery.xls* and keep the file open for the next task.

Your solution should be similar to this

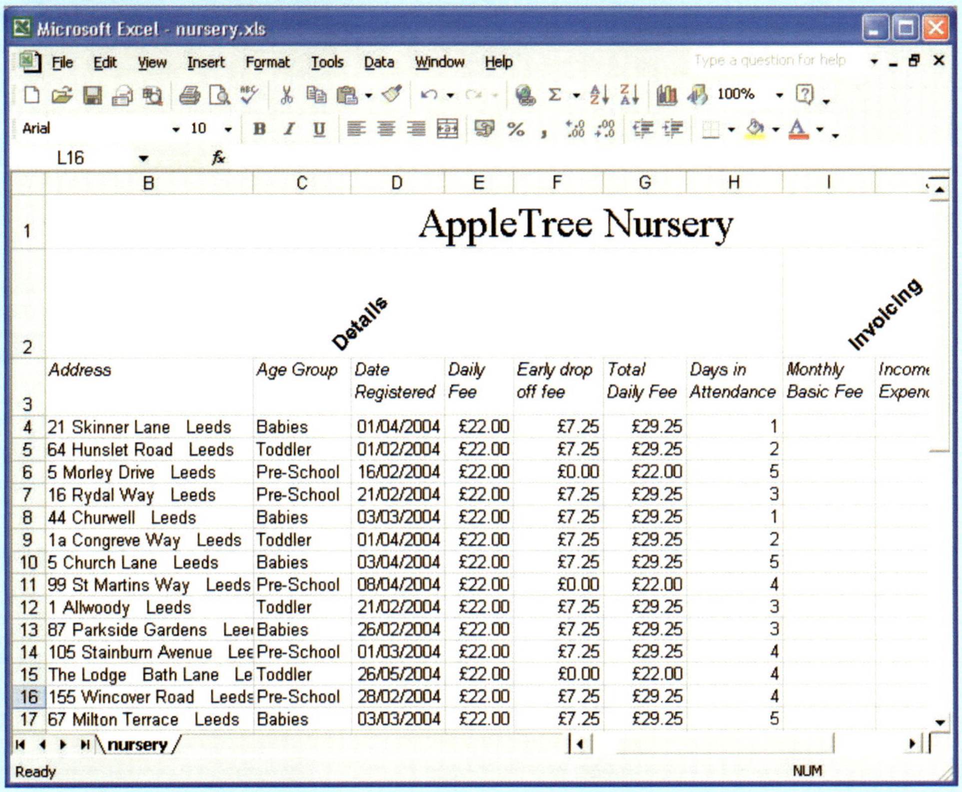

Microsoft Excel - nursery.xls

	B	C	D	E	F	G	H	I	
1	AppleTree Nursery								
2		Details						Invoicing	
3	Address	Age Group	Date Registered	Daily Fee	Early drop off fee	Total Daily Fee	Days in Attendance	Monthly Basic Fee	Income Expen
4	21 Skinner Lane Leeds	Babies	01/04/2004	£22.00	£7.25	£29.25	1		
5	64 Hunslet Road Leeds	Toddler	01/02/2004	£22.00	£7.25	£29.25	2		
6	5 Morley Drive Leeds	Pre-School	16/02/2004	£22.00	£0.00	£22.00	5		
7	16 Rydal Way Leeds	Pre-School	21/02/2004	£22.00	£7.25	£29.25	3		
8	44 Churwell Leeds	Babies	03/03/2004	£22.00	£7.25	£29.25	1		
9	1a Congreve Way Leeds	Toddler	01/04/2004	£22.00	£7.25	£29.25	2		
10	5 Church Lane Leeds	Babies	03/04/2004	£22.00	£7.25	£29.25	5		
11	99 St Martins Way Leeds	Pre-School	08/04/2004	£22.00	£0.00	£22.00	4		
12	1 Allwoody Leeds	Toddler	21/02/2004	£22.00	£7.25	£29.25	3		
13	87 Parkside Gardens Lee	Babies	26/02/2004	£22.00	£7.25	£29.25	3		
14	105 Stainburn Avenue Lee	Pre-School	01/03/2004	£22.00	£7.25	£29.25	4		
15	The Lodge Bath Lane Le	Toddler	26/05/2004	£22.00	£0.00	£22.00	4		
16	155 Wincover Road Leeds	Pre-School	28/02/2004	£22.00	£7.25	£29.25	4		
17	67 Milton Terrace Leeds	Babies	03/03/2004	£22.00	£7.25	£29.25	5		

Combining operators in functions

When creating formulas you can combine operators. The main arithmetic operators are:

(addition)	+
(subtraction)	-
(multiplication)	*
(division)	/

- Basic concepts
- Entering and formatting data
- Basic formulas and functions
  - Introducing simple formulas
  - Entering simple formulas
  - **Combining operators in formulas**
  - Using basic functions
  - Dealing with common errors in formulas
  - Using the Function Wizard
  - Exercise on Basic formulas and functions
- Entering and organising data
- Charts
- Customising worksheets
- Advanced formulas and functions
- Distributing your worksheets

Remember that where you place the brackets in a formula affects the order in which operations are calculated.

Skill Builder 2.5

1 Using *nursery.xls*, in cell I4 calculate the *Monthly Basic Fee* (*Total Daily Fee* * *Days in Attendance* * 52/12). Replicate across the other records.

2 Save the file as *nursery.xls* and close it.

Your solution should be similar to this

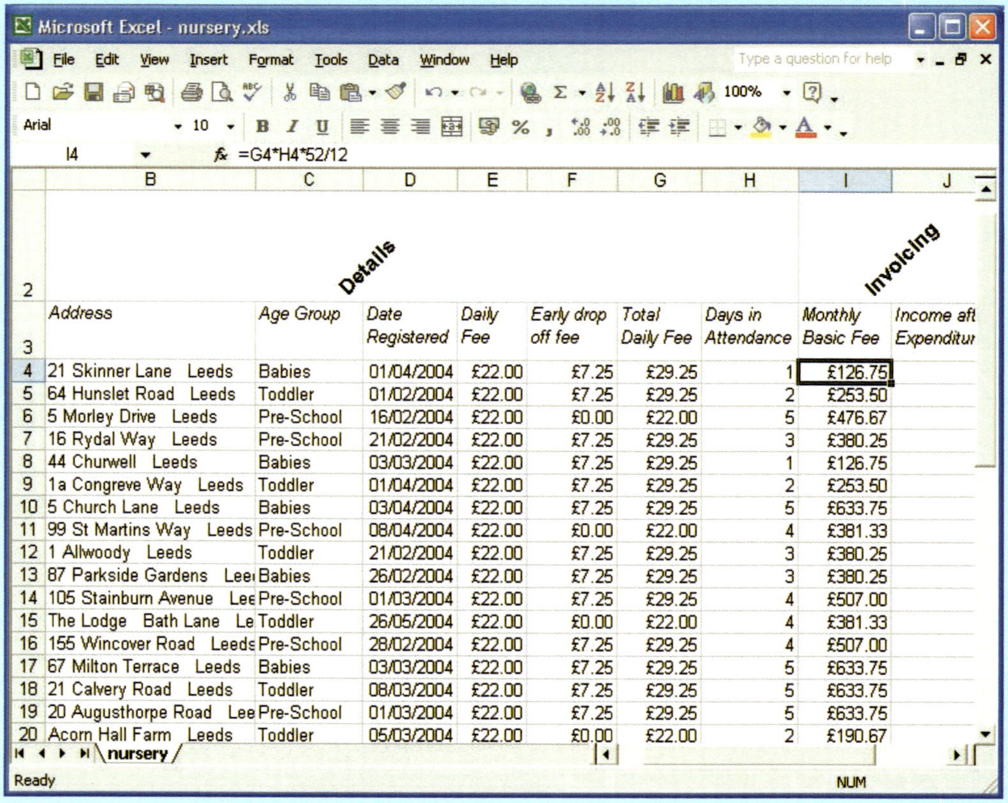
Microsoft Excel - nursery.xls

I4 =G4*H4*52/12

	B	C	D	E	F	G	H	I	J
2		Details						Invoicing	
3	Address	Age Group	Date Registered	Daily Fee	Early drop off fee	Total Daily Fee	Days in Attendance	Monthly Basic Fee	Income aft Expenditur
4	21 Skinner Lane Leeds	Babies	01/04/2004	£22.00	£7.25	£29.25	1	£126.75	
5	64 Hunslet Road Leeds	Toddler	01/02/2004	£22.00	£7.25	£29.25	2	£253.50	
6	5 Morley Drive Leeds	Pre-School	16/02/2004	£22.00	£0.00	£22.00	5	£476.67	
7	16 Rydal Way Leeds	Pre-School	21/02/2004	£22.00	£7.25	£29.25	3	£380.25	
8	44 Churwell Leeds	Babies	03/03/2004	£22.00	£7.25	£29.25	1	£126.75	
9	1a Congreve Way Leeds	Toddler	01/04/2004	£22.00	£7.25	£29.25	2	£253.50	
10	5 Church Lane Leeds	Babies	03/04/2004	£22.00	£7.25	£29.25	5	£633.75	
11	99 St Martins Way Leeds	Pre-School	08/04/2004	£22.00	£0.00	£22.00	4	£381.33	
12	1 Allwoody Leeds	Toddler	21/02/2004	£22.00	£7.25	£29.25	3	£380.25	
13	87 Parkside Gardens Lee	Babies	26/02/2004	£22.00	£7.25	£29.25	3	£380.25	
14	105 Stainburn Avenue Lee	Pre-School	01/03/2004	£22.00	£7.25	£29.25	4	£507.00	
15	The Lodge Bath Lane Le	Toddler	26/05/2004	£22.00	£0.00	£22.00	4	£381.33	
16	155 Wincover Road Leeds	Pre-School	28/02/2004	£22.00	£7.25	£29.25	4	£507.00	
17	67 Milton Terrace Leeds	Babies	03/03/2004	£22.00	£7.25	£29.25	5	£633.75	
18	21 Calvery Road Leeds	Toddler	08/03/2004	£22.00	£7.25	£29.25	5	£633.75	
19	20 Augusthorpe Road Lee	Pre-School	01/03/2004	£22.00	£7.25	£29.25	5	£633.75	
20	Acorn Hall Farm Leeds	Toddler	05/03/2004	£22.00	£0.00	£22.00	2	£190.67	

nursery

Ready NUM

Using the Function Wizard

In the next Skill Builder you will use the Function Wizard to calculate the average monthly income.

- Basic concepts
- Entering and formatting data
- Basic formulas and functions
  - Introducing simple formulas
  - Entering simple formulas
  - Combining operators in formulas
  - Using basic functions
  - Dealing with common errors in formulas
  - Using the Function Wizard
  - Exercise on Basic formulas and functions
- Entering and organising data
- Charts
- Customising worksheets
- Advanced formulas and functions
- Distributing your worksheets

Skill Builder **2.6**

1 Open the *nursery.xls* spreadsheet.

2 In the Summary Figures section calculate the *Total monthly income* by adding together all the fees in the *Monthly Basic Fee* column.

3 In the Summary Figures section calculate the *Yearly income* by multiplying the *Total monthly income* by the number of *months* (from the Fee Structure part of the spreadsheet).

4 In the Summary Figures section calculate the *Average Monthly Fee*.

5 Click the Function Wizard button. In the dialogue box select **Average** from the list and click **OK**.

6 Select the data in the *Monthly Basic Fee* column as shown below.

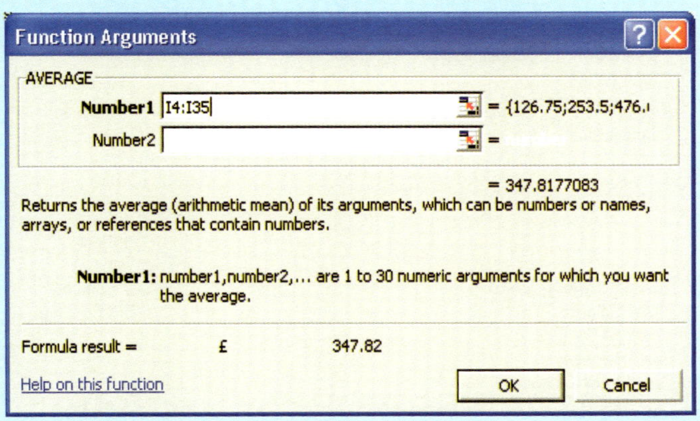

7 Click **OK** and the result £347.82 is shown.

8 Save the spreadsheet as *nursery.xls* and close the file.

Entering and organising data

Moving, duplicating and copying data

Data can easily be edited and organized using the Cut/Copy and Paste tools. Cut or Copied data is stored on the Clipboard until you exit the application when you will be prompted to clear or save it.

- Basic concepts
- Entering and formatting data
- Basic formulas and functions
- Entering and organising data
- Charts
- Customising worksheets
- Advanced formulas and functions
- Distributing your worksheets

- Editing cell contents
- Moving and duplicating data
- Using the Office clipboard
- Deleting cells, rows and columns
- Inserting cells, rows and columns
- Reorganising your worksheets
- Using proofreading tools
- Sorting data
- Exercise on Editing and organising data
- Task on Editing and organising data

Skill Builder 2.7

1 Open the spreadsheet file *courses.xls*.

2 Copy the data in the cells O3 to P6.

3 Paste the data into cells E25 to F28.

4 Save file as *paste* and close the file.

Your solution should be similar to this

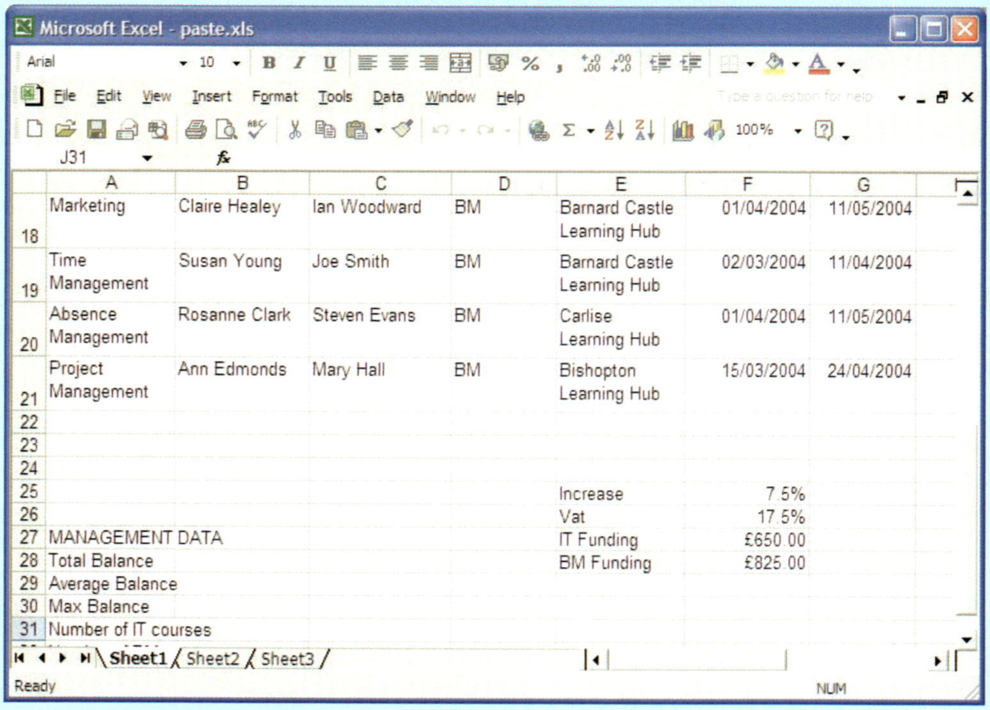

	A	B	C	D	E	F	G
18	Marketing	Claire Healey	Ian Woodward	BM	Barnard Castle Learning Hub	01/04/2004	11/05/2004
19	Time Management	Susan Young	Joe Smith	BM	Barnard Castle Learning Hub	02/03/2004	11/04/2004
20	Absence Management	Rosanne Clark	Steven Evans	BM	Carlise Learning Hub	01/04/2004	11/05/2004
21	Project Management	Ann Edmonds	Mary Hall	BM	Bishopton Learning Hub	15/03/2004	24/04/2004
22							
23							
24							
25					Increase	7.5%	
26					Vat	17.5%	
27	MANAGEMENT DATA				IT Funding	£650.00	
28	Total Balance				BM Funding	£825.00	
29	Average Balance						
30	Max Balance						
31	Number of IT courses						

Office 2000 – to open the Office toolbar, select **View > Toolbars > Office Clipboard.** Office XP – select **Edit > Office Clipboard.**

Deleting and inserting cells, rows and columns

When deleting a row from the spreadsheet, remember that the row itself and its data needs to be deleted and not just the data in the cells.

When inserting columns/rows, position them carefully. Any additional data should be entered as instructed. It will usually follow a set pattern, e.g. ascending product code order.

- Basic concepts
- Entering and formatting data
- Basic formulas and functions
- Entering and organising data
  - Editing cell contents
  - Moving and duplicating data
  - Using the Office clipboard
  - **Deleting cells, rows and columns**
  - **Inserting cells, rows and columns**
  - Reorganising your worksheets
  - Using proofreading tools
  - Sorting data
  - Exercise on Editing and organising data
  - Task on Editing and organising data
- Charts
- Customising worksheets
- Advanced formulas and functions
- Distributing your worksheets

Skill Builder **2.8**

1 Open the *nursery.xls* file.

2 Delete all data for Susan Clements.

3 Add the following data

Name Joe Clarke	**Address** 6 Skinner Lane Leeds
Age Group Babies	**Date Registered** 21/02/2004
Days in Attendance 3	
Daily Fee £22.00	**Early Drop Off fee** £0.00

Name Sarah Smith	**Address** 6 Augusthorpe Road Leeds
Age Group Toddler	**Date Registered** 05/04/04
Days in Attendance 5	
Daily Fee £22.00	**Early Drop Off fee** £0.00

4 Ensure that the formulas are replicated over the new rows and that the totals have been updated.

5 Save the spreadsheet as *nursery.xls* and close the file.

Sorting data

In the following Skill Builder you will sort the spreadsheet into ascending order whilst maintaining data integrity. This means that when you sort one column all the remaining data is moved accordingly and the data does not become muddled.

- Basic concepts
- Entering and formatting data
- Basic formulas and functions
- Entering and organising data
  - Editing cell contents
  - Moving and duplicating data
  - Using the Office clipboard
  - Deleting cells, rows and columns
  - Inserting cells, rows and columns
  - **Reorganising your worksheets**
  - **Using proofreading tools**
  - **Sorting data**
  - Exercise on Editing and organising data
  - Task on Editing and organising data
- Charts
- Customising worksheets
- Advanced formulas and functions
- Distributing your worksheets

Skill Builder **2.9**

1 Using the *nursery.xls* spreadsheet sort the data into ascending order of *Days in Attendance.*

2 Save the spreadsheet as *nursery.xls* and close the file.

Your solution should be similar to this

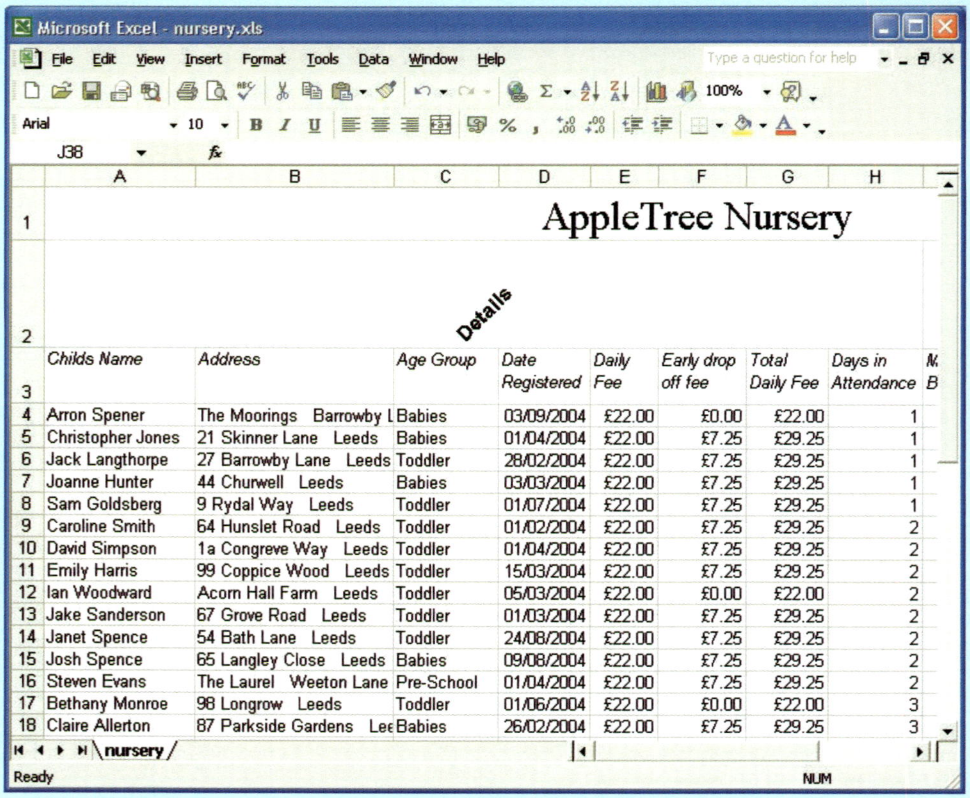

AppleTree Nursery

Details

	Childs Name	Address	Age Group	Date Registered	Daily Fee	Early drop off fee	Total Daily Fee	Days in Attendance
4	Arron Spener	The Moorings Barrowby L	Babies	03/09/2004	£22.00	£0.00	£22.00	1
5	Christopher Jones	21 Skinner Lane Leeds	Babies	01/04/2004	£22.00	£7.25	£29.25	1
6	Jack Langthorpe	27 Barrowby Lane Leeds	Toddler	28/02/2004	£22.00	£7.25	£29.25	1
7	Joanne Hunter	44 Churwell Leeds	Babies	03/03/2004	£22.00	£7.25	£29.25	1
8	Sam Goldsberg	9 Rydal Way Leeds	Toddler	01/07/2004	£22.00	£7.25	£29.25	1
9	Caroline Smith	64 Hunslet Road Leeds	Toddler	01/02/2004	£22.00	£7.25	£29.25	2
10	David Simpson	1a Congreve Way Leeds	Toddler	01/04/2004	£22.00	£7.25	£29.25	2
11	Emily Harris	99 Coppice Wood Leeds	Toddler	15/03/2004	£22.00	£7.25	£29.25	2
12	Ian Woodward	Acorn Hall Farm Leeds	Toddler	05/03/2004	£22.00	£0.00	£22.00	2
13	Jake Sanderson	67 Grove Road Leeds	Toddler	01/03/2004	£22.00	£7.25	£29.25	2
14	Janet Spence	54 Bath Lane Leeds	Toddler	24/08/2004	£22.00	£7.25	£29.25	2
15	Josh Spence	65 Langley Close Leeds	Babies	09/08/2004	£22.00	£7.25	£29.25	2
16	Steven Evans	The Laurel Weeton Lane	Pre-School	01/04/2004	£22.00	£7.25	£29.25	2
17	Bethany Monroe	98 Longrow Leeds	Toddler	01/06/2004	£22.00	£0.00	£22.00	3
18	Claire Allerton	87 Parkside Gardens Lee	Babies	26/02/2004	£22.00	£7.25	£29.25	3

In the assignments, failure to maintain data integrity when sorting is penalised as a critical error

Mini Assignment 2.2

1 Open the *courses.xls* spreadsheet and ensure that all data is shown in full.

2 Calculate the *Balance* by subtracting the *Tutor Fee* from the *Cost*.

3 In the Management Data section calculate the *Max Balance* by using the Function Wizard. Your formula will begin =MAX

4 Sort the spreadsheet data into ascending order of *Start Date*.

5 The Marketing course is not proving to be profitable and therefore this should be withdrawn from the spreadsheet.

6 Ensure that all formulas have been updated.

7 Save the file as *coursesa.xls* and close the file.

Your solution should be similar to this

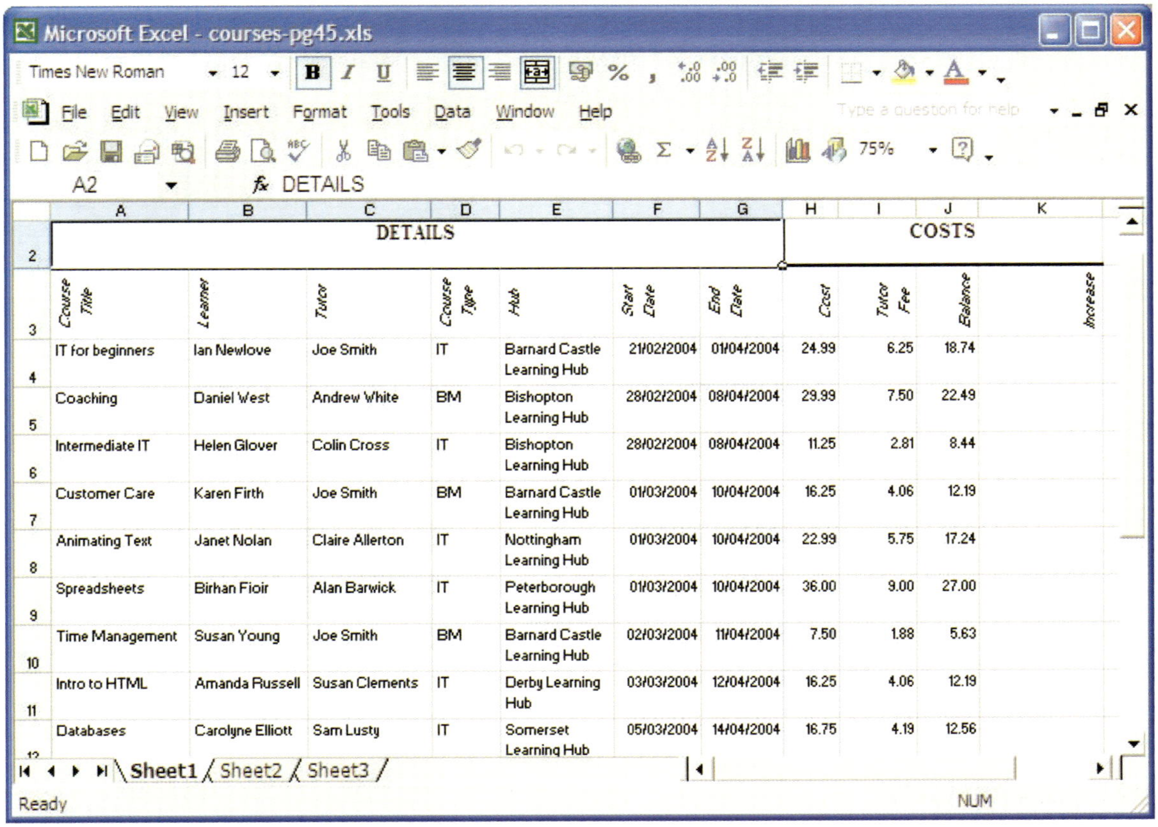

	DETAILS							COSTS			
	Course Title	Learner	Tutor	Course Type	Hub	Start Date	End Date	Cost	Tutor Fee	Balance	Increase
4	IT for beginners	Ian Newlove	Joe Smith	IT	Barnard Castle Learning Hub	21/02/2004	01/04/2004	24.99	6.25	18.74	
5	Coaching	Daniel West	Andrew White	BM	Bishopton Learning Hub	28/02/2004	08/04/2004	29.99	7.50	22.49	
6	Intermediate IT	Helen Glover	Colin Cross	IT	Bishopton Learning Hub	28/02/2004	08/04/2004	11.25	2.81	8.44	
7	Customer Care	Karen Firth	Joe Smith	BM	Barnard Castle Learning Hub	01/03/2004	10/04/2004	16.25	4.06	12.19	
8	Animating Text	Janet Nolan	Claire Allerton	IT	Nottingham Learning Hub	01/03/2004	10/04/2004	22.99	5.75	17.24	
9	Spreadsheets	Birhan Fioir	Alan Barwick	IT	Peterborough Learning Hub	01/03/2004	10/04/2004	36.00	9.00	27.00	
10	Time Management	Susan Young	Joe Smith	BM	Barnard Castle Learning Hub	02/03/2004	11/04/2004	7.50	1.88	5.63	
11	Intro to HTML	Amanda Russell	Susan Clements	IT	Derby Learning Hub	03/03/2004	12/04/2004	16.25	4.06	12.19	
12	Databases	Carolyne Elliott	Sam Lusty	IT	Somerset Learning Hub	05/03/2004	14/04/2004	16.75	4.19	12.56	

Charts

Types of charts

In Excel you can produce different graphs and charts to suit the data. The e-course covers pie charts, comparative bar charts, scatter graphs and line-column graphs. In the CLAIT Plus exam you will also have to create an exploded pie chart and one XY (scatter) graph with a trend line and another where the plots are joined.

- Basic concepts
- Entering and formatting data
- Basic formulas and functions
- Entering and organising data
- Charts
  - **What is a chart?**
  - Selecting the data for your chart
  - Choosing the appropriate chart for your data
  - Microsoft Excel's Chart Wizard
  - Working with the Chart toolbar
  - Formatting individual parts of a chart
  - Manipulating charts
  - Working with scatter charts
  - Exercise on Charts
  - Task on Charts
- Customising worksheets
- Advanced formulas and functions
- Distributing your worksheets

Pie chart

A pie chart is a circle which represents the total of all of the values in a series. Each item of data is represented by a number of degrees. These can be converted into percentages allowing the data to be analysed more easily. In an exploded pie chart, none of the segments touch, and you can highlight a segment by pulling it further out from the centre.

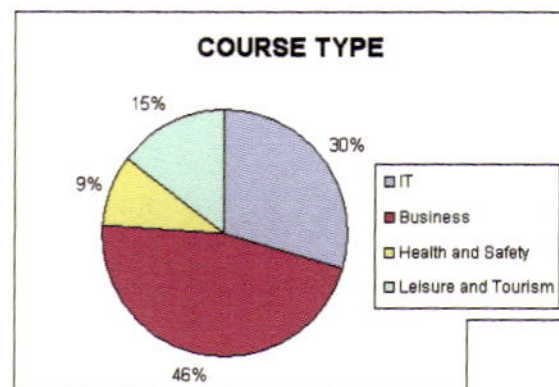

A plain pie chart...

...an exploded pie

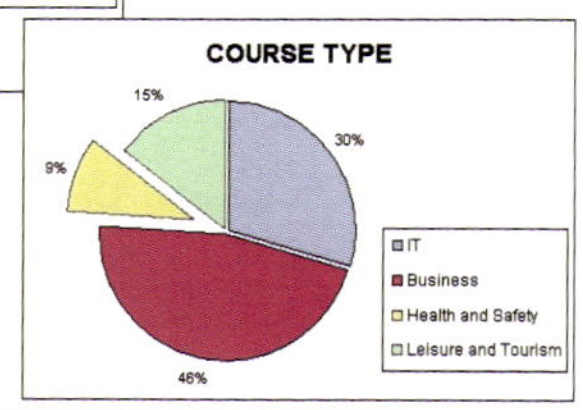

Comparative bar chart

A bar chart uses columns to represent values on two axes, the x axis (horizontal) and the y axis (vertical). A comparative bar chart contains more than one bar for each set of data so that comparisons can be made.

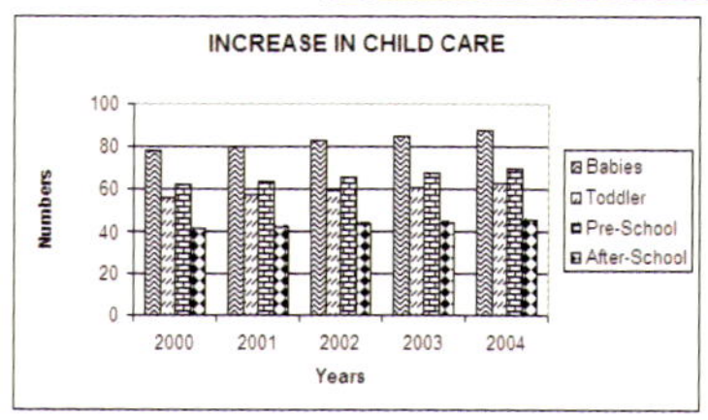

XY (scatter) graph

XY (scatter) graphs display observations showing the values of two variables, one dependent and one independent. The plot points can be joined together, or a trendline and its equation can be added.

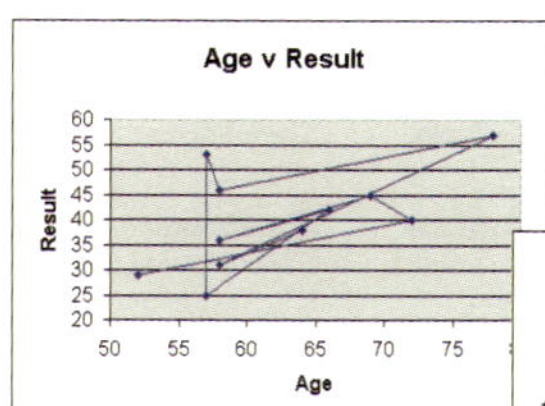

XY (scatter) graphs, with joining lines ...

...with a trendline

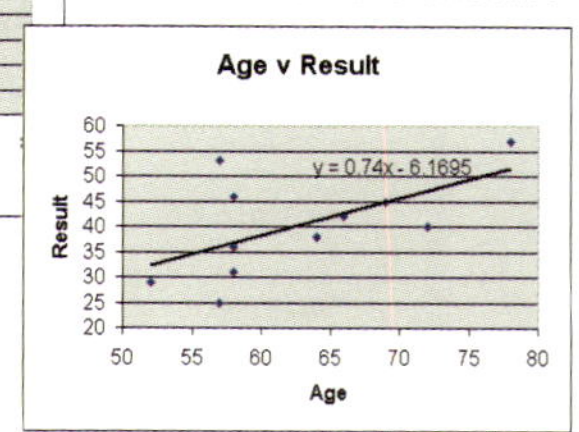

Line – column graph

A line – column graph allows two different chart types to be used to display the data, e.g. projected sales can be shown as columns whereas actual sales can be shown as a line.

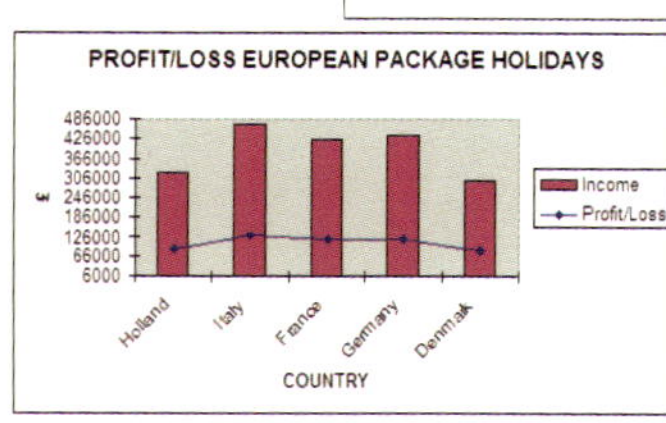

Using the Chart Wizard

In this section you will create five different charts using data provided. Creating charts is not usually difficult but you must ensure that you select the correct data to be displayed on each axis.

First you will create a pie chart.

- Basic concepts
- Entering and formatting data
- Basic formulas and functions
- Entering and organising data
- Charts
  - What is a chart?
  - **Selecting the data for your chart**
  - **Choosing the appropriate chart for your data**
  - **Microsoft Excel's Chart Wizard**
  - Working with the Chart toolbar
  - Formatting individual parts of a chart
  - Manipulating charts
  - Working with scatter charts
  - Exercise on Charts
  - Task on Charts
- Customising worksheets
- Advanced formulas and functions
- Distributing your worksheets

Skill Builder **2.10**

1 Using the file *pie.xls* create a pie chart to show the percentage of learners on each type of course that we offer.

2 Select the *Course Type* and *Number of Learners* from the spreadsheet. **Do not include the data for the Key Skills learners.**

3 Enter the title:
PERCENTAGE OF LEARNERS PER COURSE

4 Show the percentages for each segment.

5 Create the chart as a new sheet.

6 Save the file as *percentage.xls*.

Your solution should be similar to this

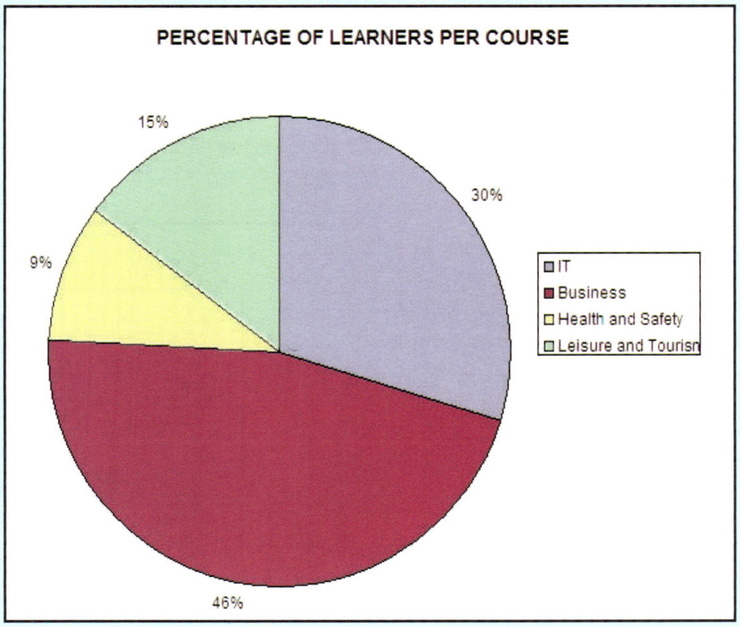

Exploded pie charts

In the CLAIT Plus assessment you are required to create an exploded pie chart. Here's how to do it.

1 Select your data and start the Chart Wizard. Work through the Wizard as normal, but setting these options. At step 1, select **Pie**, then the first exploded pie chart from the second row.

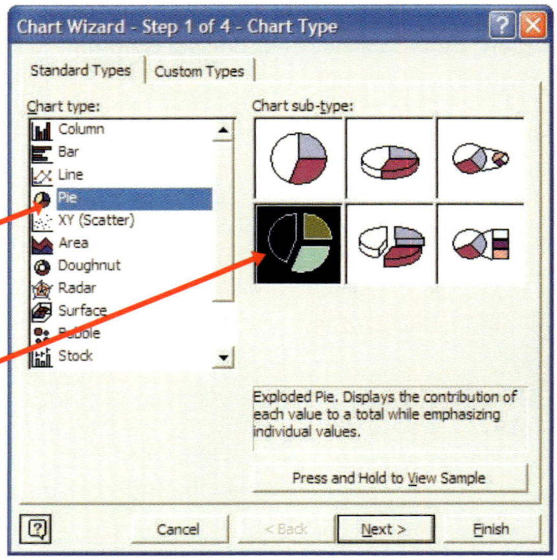

Select Pie…

…then the 2-D exploded type

2 At step 3, go to the **Data Labels** tab and select what to show on the labels.

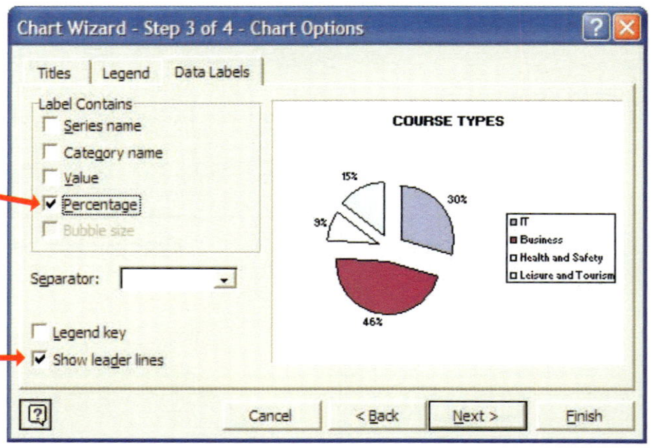

Percentage is the most common choice for labels

Leader lines can be drawn to link labels to narrow segments

3 Once the pie chart is displayed in the sheet, you can emphasise a segment by pulling it away from the rest. Click *twice* on the segment (so that only this one shows the selection handles) then drag it away from the others.

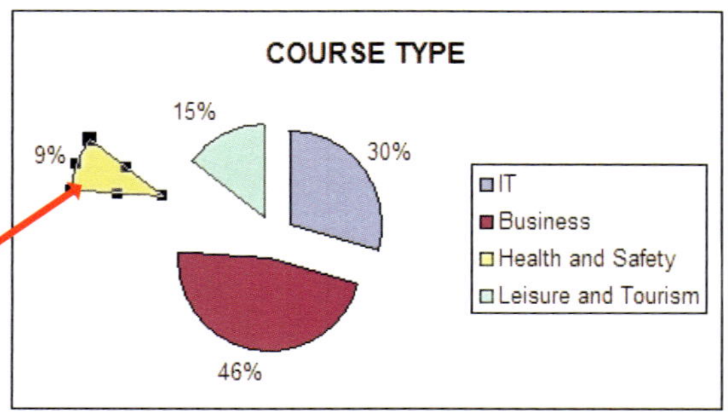

Drag a slice out of the pie to emphasise it

Working with the Chart toolbar

The Chart toolbar allows you to select data in the chart and amend it, for example you can change the title.

- Basic concepts
- Entering and formatting data
- Basic formulas and functions
- Entering and organising data
- Charts
  - What is a chart?
  - Selecting the data for your chart
  - Choosing the appropriate chart for your data
  - Microsoft Excel's Chart Wizard
  - **Working with the Chart toolbar**
  - Formatting individual parts of a chart
  - Manipulating charts
  - Working with scatter charts
  - Exercise on Charts
  - Task on Charts
- Customising worksheets
- Advanced formulas and functions
- Distributing your worksheets

Skill Builder **2.11**

1 Open the *percentage.xls* spreadsheet and click in the chart title.

2 Amend the title to read % OF LEARNERS PER COURSE.

3 Save the spreadsheet and close the file.

Skill Builder **2.12**

1 Using the *child.xls* spreadsheet create a comparative bar chart to show the increase in nursery places over the past 5 years.

2 Title the chart: INCREASE IN CHILD CARE

3 Enter the x-axis label Years and the y-axis label Numbers.

4 Show a legend to represent the bars in the chart.

5 Save the chart as *child.xls* and close the file.

Your solution should be similar to this

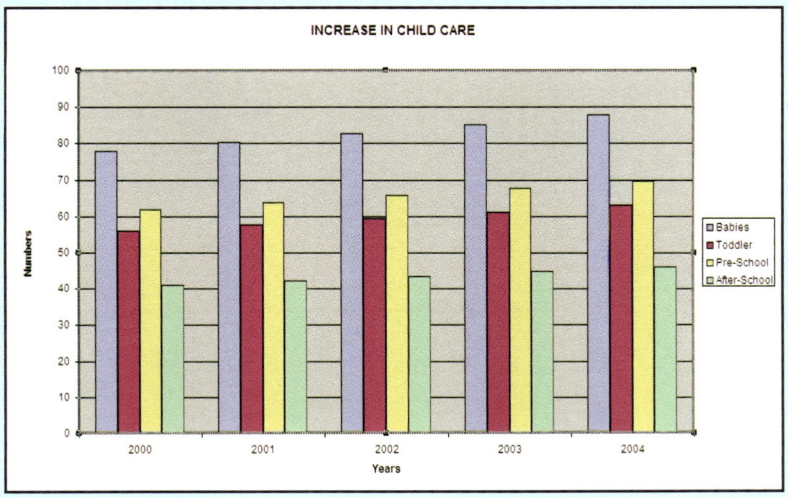

Formatting individual parts of a chart

In this Skill Builder you will amend the comparative bar chart, changing the fill effects and the colour of the data series.

- Basic concepts
- Entering and formatting data
- Basic formulas and functions
- Entering and organising data
- Charts
- Customising worksheets
- Advanced formulas and functions
- Distributing your worksheets

- What is a chart?
- Selecting the data for your chart
- Choosing the appropriate chart for your data
- Microsoft Excel's Chart Wizard
- Working with the Chart toolbar
- Formatting individual parts of a chart
- Manipulating charts
- Working with scatter charts
- Exercise on Charts
- Task on Charts

Skill Builder **2.13**

1 Open the *child.xls* comparative bar chart.

2 Right-click in the plot area (the background to the bars) and select **Format Plot Area**. Change the plot area to be white.

3 Select all the bars within the *Babies* category and change the fill effects to zig zag with a black foreground and white background. You can double-click on the bars to open the **Format Data Series** dialogue box.

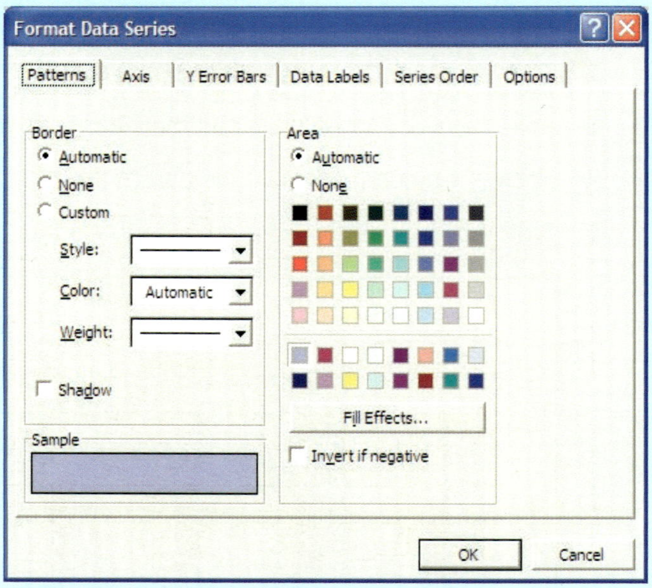

4 Click on **Fill Effects**. The **Fill Effects** dialogue box appears (see the next page). Switch to the **Patterns** tab.

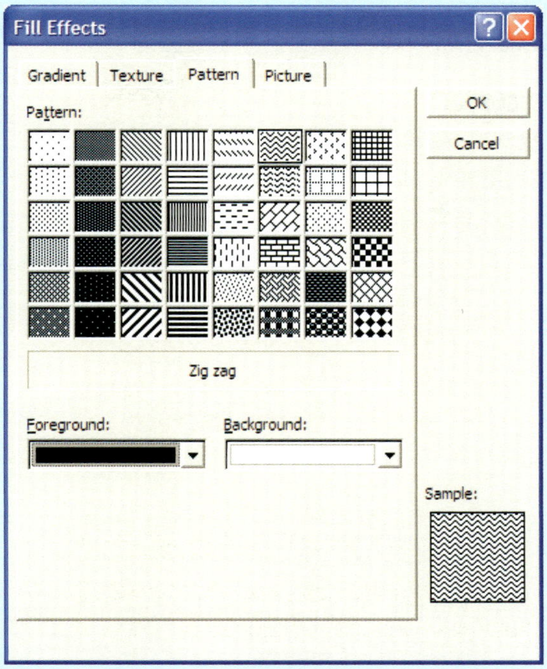

5 Click **OK** twice. Repeat this process for the remaining bars using different patterns.

6 Save the chart as *child.xls* and close the file.

Your solution should be similar to this

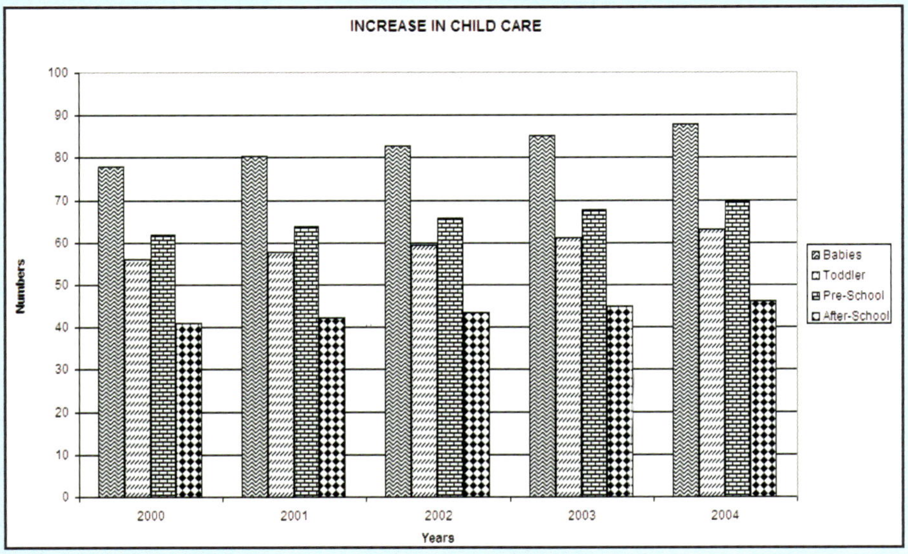

Manipulating charts

The following Skill Builder allows you to practise changing the labels and scales on a graph. This can make a graph easier to read.

- Basic concepts
- Entering and formatting data
- Basic formulas and functions
- Entering and organising data
- Charts
  - What is a chart?
  - Selecting the data for your chart
  - Choosing the appropriate chart for your data
  - Microsoft Excel's Chart Wizard
  - Working with the Chart toolbar
  - Formatting individual parts of a chart
  - **Manipulating charts**
  - Working with scatter charts
  - Exercise on Charts
  - Task on Charts
- Customising worksheets
- Advanced formulas and functions
- Distributing your worksheets

Skill Builder **2.14**

1. Open the file *hols.csv* and create a line – column graph to plot the *Income from package holidays to Europe* against the *Profit/Loss.*
2. Enter the title: Profit/Loss of European Package Holidays.
   x-axis label: Country
   y-axis label: £
3. Display a legend showing: Income and Profit/Loss
4. The x axis must display: Country
5. Format the y axis. Scale: minimum 6000, maximum 486000, intervals of 60000. Numbers set to 0 decimal places.
6. Set the orientation to landscape. Save the file as *line-col.xls* and close it.

Your solution should be similar to this

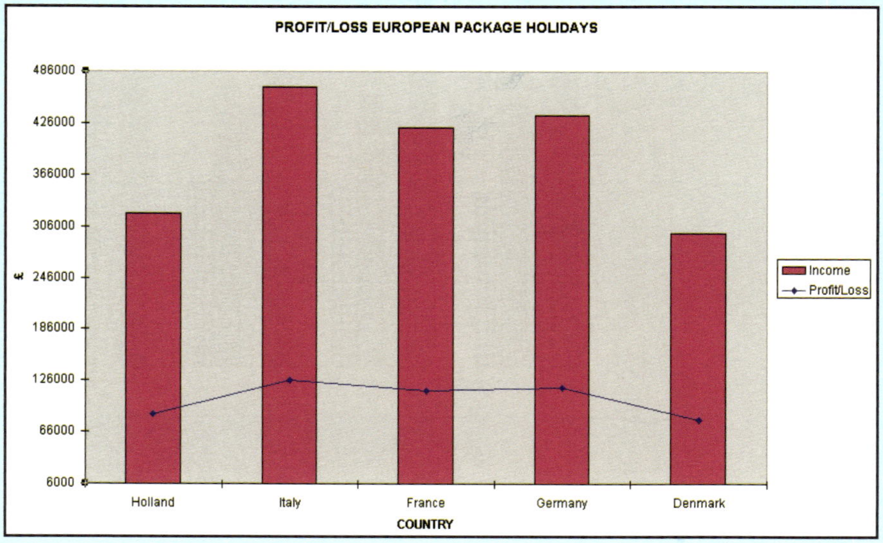

Working with scatter graphs

In this Skill Builder you will create a scatter graph. You will also open a .csv file and save it in Excel's normal file type.

- Basic concepts
- Entering and formatting data
- Basic formulas and functions
- Entering and organising data
- Charts
  - What is a chart?
  - Selecting the data for your chart
  - Choosing the appropriate chart for your data
  - Microsoft Excel's Chart Wizard
  - Working with the Chart toolbar
  - Formatting individual parts of a chart
  - Manipulating charts
  - **Working with scatter charts**
  - Exercise on Charts
  - Task on Charts
- Customising worksheets
- Advanced formulas and functions
- Distributing your worksheets

Skill Builder **2.15**

1 Open the file called *assig.csv* and save it in Excel's normal file format.

2 Create an XY (scatter) graph to plot *Age of Learners* against *Assignment Results*.

3 Title the chart: AGE –v– ASSIGNMENT RESULTS
x-axis label: AGE   y-axis label: ASSIGNMENT RESULTS

4 Do not display a legend on the graph.

5 Format the x axis. Scale: minimum value 25, maximum value 45, intervals set at 2 (years)

6 Format the y axis. Scale: minimum value 45, maximum value 90, intervals set at 5. Number format: integer (no decimal places).

7 Set the chart orientation to landscape. Save and print the graph.

Your solution should be similar to this

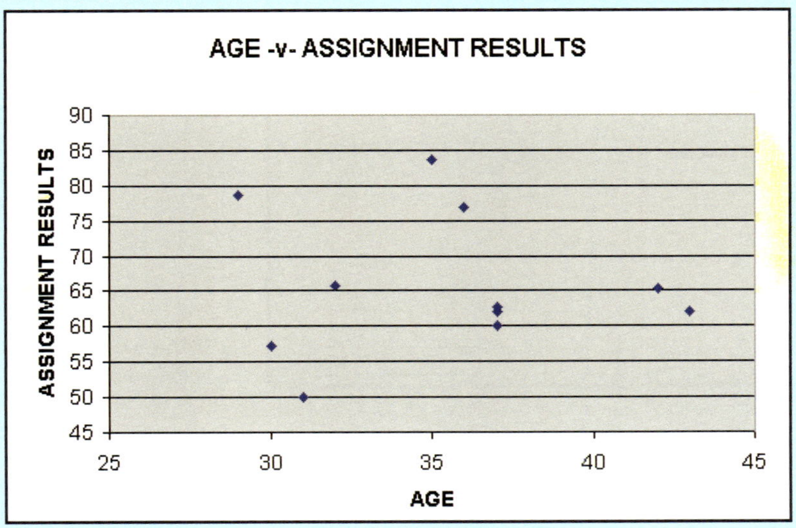

XY (scatter) graph options

Adding a trendline

A trendline can be added to a scatter graph to show trends in the data. If most of the points are close to the trendline, it shows that there is a significant relationship between the two series of values.

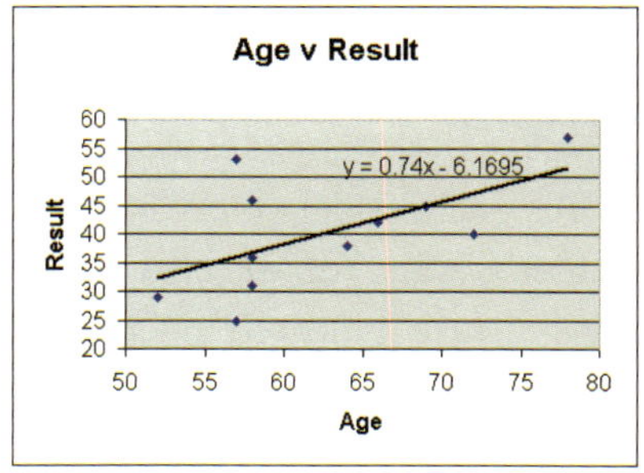

1 Create your XY (scatter) graph with the Chart Wizard.
2 When the graph is displayed, open the **Chart** menu and select **Add Trendline...**
3 At the dialogue box, select **Linear** as the **Type**.
4 Go to the **Options** tab and place a tick in the **Display equation on chart** checkbox.

Select the Linear type

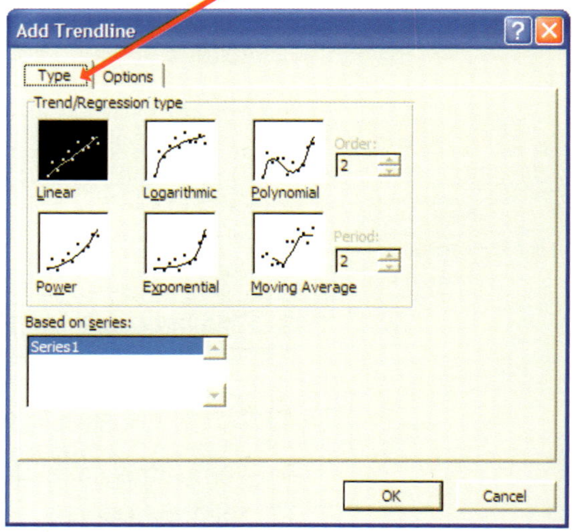

Joining the points

The points on a XY (scatter) graph can be joined by lines. You can select the joined sub-type when you create the graph, or add the lines later. To add lines:

1 Double-click on the points to open the **Format Data Series** dialogue box.

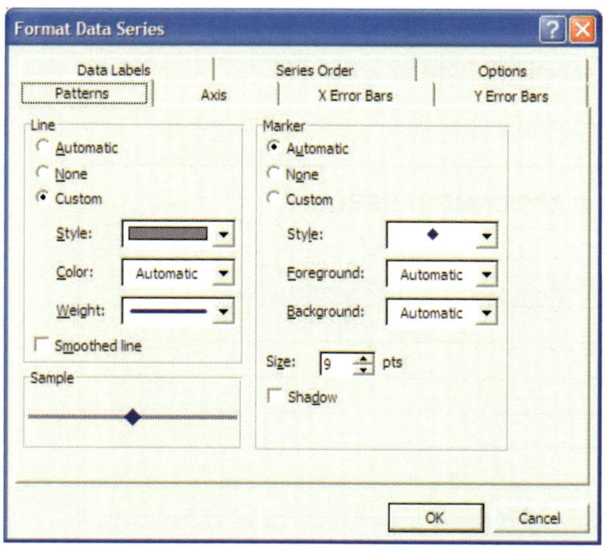

2 On the **Patterns** tab, select **Custom** in the **Line** area and set the style, colour and weight of the line.
3 Click **OK**.

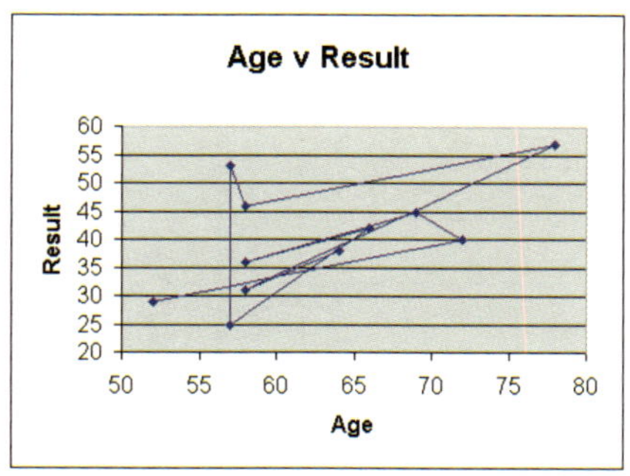

If the data is first sorted into order of the x axis value, it can make any relationships clearer

Mini Assignment 2.3

1 Open the file called *result.csv* and save it in Excel's normal file format.

2 Create an XY (scatter) graph to plot *Age* against *Results*.

3 Title the chart: AGE –v- RESULTS

x-axis label: AGE y-axis label: RESULTS

4 Do not display a legend on the graph.

5 Format the x axis. Scale: minimum value 25, maximum value 60, intervals set at 5.

6 Format the y axis. Scale: minimum value 45, maximum value 90, intervals set at 5.

7 Add a linear trendline to the graph and display the equation of the trendline in the plot area.

8 Format the trendline so that it appears as a thick solid line.

9 Format the markers so that they appear as triangles and size 12.

10 Change the plot area to white.

11 Set the chart orientation to landscape.

12 Save and print the graph.

Your solution should be similar to this

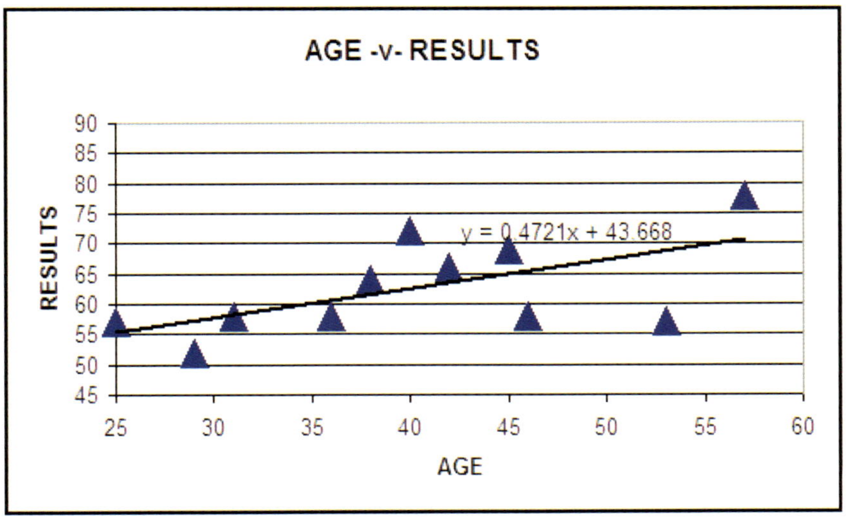

It is imperative that data is displayed on the correct axis – if the x axis data is incorrectly plotted on the y axis this is penalised as a critical error.

Customising worksheets

Naming cells and ranges

Named cells can help to make your formulas more readable.

- Basic concepts
- Entering and formatting data
- Basic formulas and functions
- Entering and organising data
- Charts
- Customising worksheets
  - **Working with more than one window**
  - **Splitting a worksheet**
  - **Freezing parts of a worksheet**
  - **Naming cells and ranges**
  - Hiding spreadsheet data
  - Exercise on Customising worksheet
- Advanced formulas and functions
- Distributing your worksheets

Skill Builder **2.16**

1 Open *nursery.xls* and name the cell holding the Percentage Profit as *profit*.

2 Name the cell containing the number of months (12) as *months*.

3 Calculate the Income after Expenditure by multiplying *Monthly Basic Fee* by *Months* and multiply this by *Percentage Profit* in the Fee Structure section.

4 Replicate this formula for all other clients.

5 Save the spreadsheet as *nursery.xls* and close the file.

Your solution should be similar to this

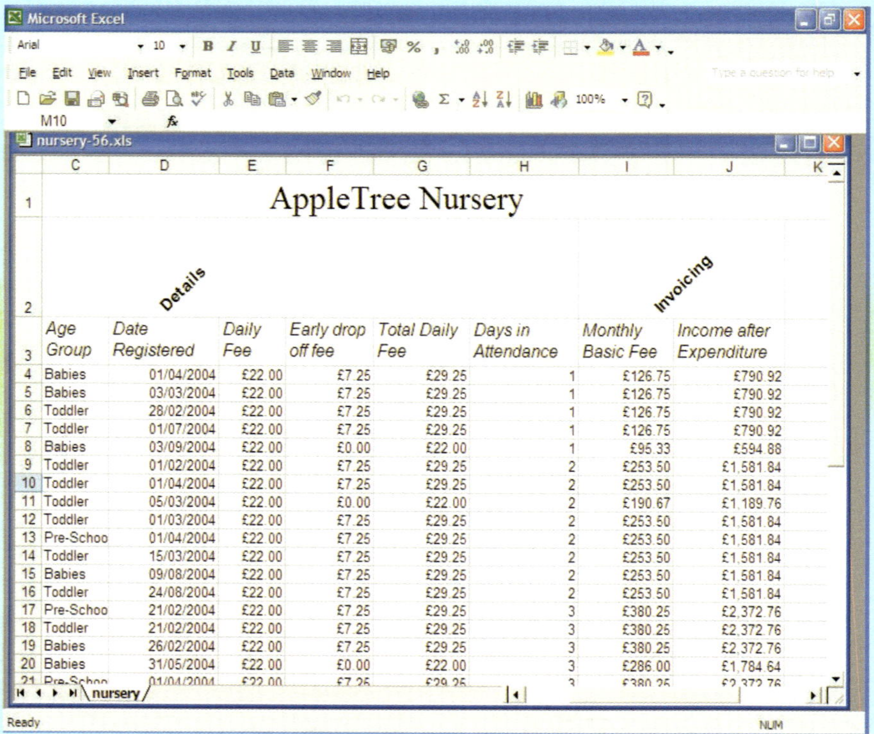

	Age Group	Date Registered	Daily Fee	Early drop off fee	Total Daily Fee	Days in Attendance	Monthly Basic Fee	Income after Expenditure
4	Babies	01/04/2004	£22.00	£7.25	£29.25	1	£126.75	£790.92
5	Babies	03/03/2004	£22.00	£7.25	£29.25	1	£126.75	£790.92
6	Toddler	28/02/2004	£22.00	£7.25	£29.25	1	£126.75	£790.92
7	Toddler	01/07/2004	£22.00	£7.25	£29.25	1	£126.75	£790.92
8	Babies	03/09/2004	£22.00	£0.00	£22.00	1	£95.33	£594.88
9	Toddler	01/02/2004	£22.00	£7.25	£29.25	2	£253.50	£1,581.84
10	Toddler	01/04/2004	£22.00	£7.25	£29.25	2	£253.50	£1,581.84
11	Toddler	05/03/2004	£22.00	£0.00	£22.00	2	£190.67	£1,189.76
12	Toddler	01/03/2004	£22.00	£7.25	£29.25	2	£253.50	£1,581.84
13	Pre-Schoo	01/04/2004	£22.00	£7.25	£29.25	2	£253.50	£1,581.84
14	Toddler	15/03/2004	£22.00	£7.25	£29.25	2	£253.50	£1,581.84
15	Babies	09/08/2004	£22.00	£7.25	£29.25	2	£253.50	£1,581.84
16	Toddler	24/08/2004	£22.00	£7.25	£29.25	2	£253.50	£1,581.84
17	Pre-Schoo	21/02/2004	£22.00	£7.25	£29.25	3	£380.25	£2,372.76
18	Toddler	21/02/2004	£22.00	£7.25	£29.25	3	£380.25	£2,372.76
19	Babies	26/02/2004	£22.00	£7.25	£29.25	3	£380.25	£2,372.76
20	Babies	31/05/2004	£22.00	£0.00	£22.00	3	£286.00	£1,784.64
21	Pre-Schoo	01/04/2004	£22.00	£7.25	£29.25	3	£380.25	£2,372.76

Hiding spreadsheet data

In this Skill Builder you will hide spreadsheet data so that selective printing can take place.

- Basic concepts
- Entering and formatting data
- Basic formulas and functions
- Entering and organising data
- Charts
- Customising worksheets
  - Working with more than one window
  - Splitting a worksheet
  - Freezing parts of a worksheet
  - Naming cells and ranges
  - **Hiding spreadsheet data**
  - Exercise on Customising worksheet
- Advanced formulas and functions
- Distributing your worksheets

Skill Builder 2.17

1 Open the *nursery.xls* spreadsheet and locate the *Address* and *Age Group* columns.

2 Highlight both columns and select **Format > Column > Hide**. Both columns will now disappear from view.

3 Save and close the file.

Your solution should be similar to this

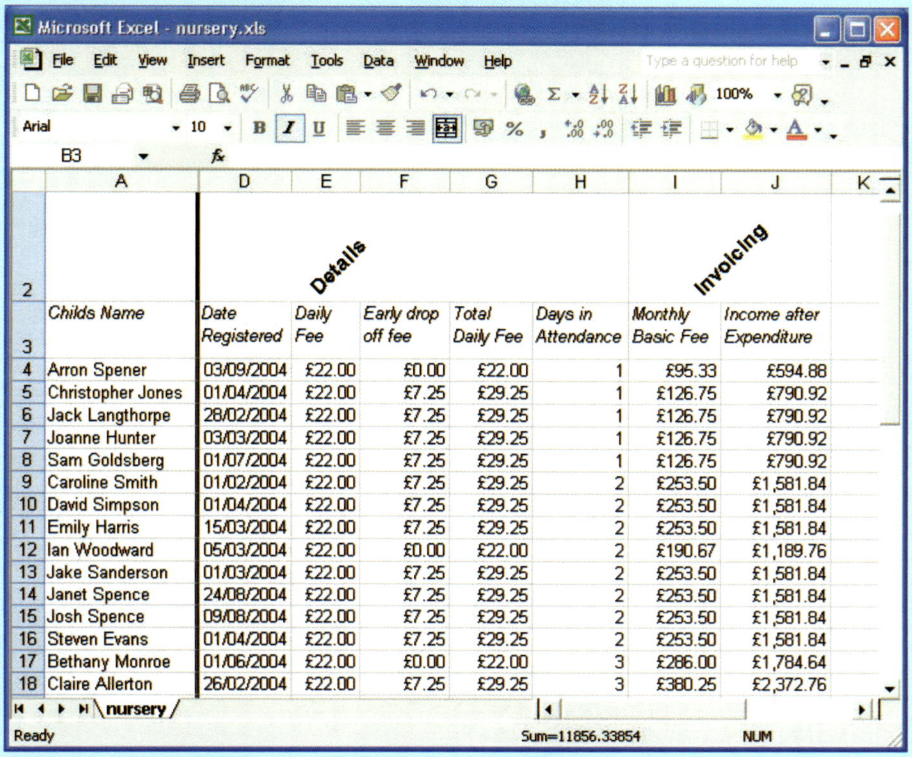

	A	D	E	F	G	H	I	J
2		Details					Invoicing	
3	*Childs Name*	*Date Registered*	*Daily Fee*	*Early drop off fee*	*Total Daily Fee*	*Days in Attendance*	*Monthly Basic Fee*	*Income after Expenditure*
4	Arron Spener	03/09/2004	£22.00	£0.00	£22.00	1	£95.33	£594.88
5	Christopher Jones	01/04/2004	£22.00	£7.25	£29.25	1	£126.75	£790.92
6	Jack Langthorpe	28/02/2004	£22.00	£7.25	£29.25	1	£126.75	£790.92
7	Joanne Hunter	03/03/2004	£22.00	£7.25	£29.25	1	£126.75	£790.92
8	Sam Goldsberg	01/07/2004	£22.00	£7.25	£29.25	1	£126.75	£790.92
9	Caroline Smith	01/02/2004	£22.00	£7.25	£29.25	2	£253.50	£1,581.84
10	David Simpson	01/04/2004	£22.00	£7.25	£29.25	2	£253.50	£1,581.84
11	Emily Harris	15/03/2004	£22.00	£7.25	£29.25	2	£253.50	£1,581.84
12	Ian Woodward	05/03/2004	£22.00	£0.00	£22.00	2	£190.67	£1,189.76
13	Jake Sanderson	01/03/2004	£22.00	£7.25	£29.25	2	£253.50	£1,581.84
14	Janet Spence	24/08/2004	£22.00	£7.25	£29.25	2	£253.50	£1,581.84
15	Josh Spence	09/08/2004	£22.00	£7.25	£29.25	2	£253.50	£1,581.84
16	Steven Evans	01/04/2004	£22.00	£7.25	£29.25	2	£253.50	£1,581.84
17	Bethany Monroe	01/06/2004	£22.00	£0.00	£22.00	3	£286.00	£1,784.64
18	Claire Allerton	26/02/2004	£22.00	£7.25	£29.25	3	£380.25	£2,372.76

Advanced formulas and functions

Relative and absolute cell address

With a relative cell address, when you replicate a formula the cell references are automatically adjusted; e.g. if you enter the formula =A1+B1 and replicate your formula, it will be =A2+B2 etc.

You can also use absolute and mixed references in your formulas.

Basic concepts
Entering and formatting data
Basic formulas and functions
Entering and organising data
Charts
Customising worksheets
Advanced formulas and functions
Distributing your worksheets

Relative cell addresses
Absolute and mixed cell addresses
Exploring different scenarios
Linking formulas
Moving cells with formulas
Inserting cells into formulas
Deleting cells from formulas
Cells referenced by formulas
The IF function
Exercise on Advanced formulas and functions

Absolute cell references refer to locations which do not change when the formula is replicated. They are created using $ symbols, e.g. A1 always refers to A1.

Mixed references have an absolute column and relative row or absolute row and relative column address. A mixed reference is displayed as $A1, $B1, or C$4. When replicating a mixed reference, the relative part of the address changes and the absolute part does not.

Skill Builder **2.18**

1 Open the *salary.xls* spreadsheet and save it with the new filename *salarya.xls*.

2 Calculate the projected increase by multiplying the salary by the increase figure. Ensure that you use an absolute cell reference.

3 Calculate the *New Salary* by adding the *Salary* and the *Projected Increase*. Replicate for the other employees. Format all monetary amounts as currency.

4 Save the file as *salarya.xls* and close it.

Your solution should be similar to this

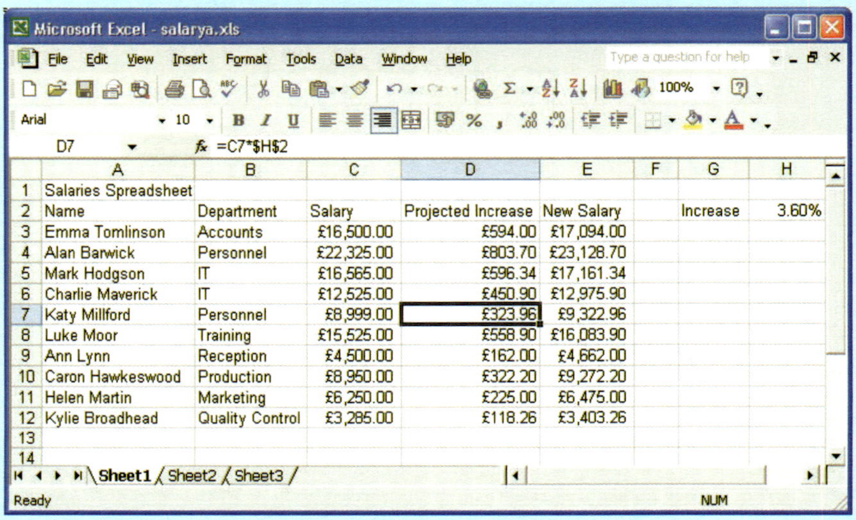

	A	B	C	D	E	F	G	H
1	Salaries Spreadsheet							
2	Name	Department	Salary	Projected Increase	New Salary		Increase	3.60%
3	Emma Tomlinson	Accounts	£16,500.00	£594.00	£17,094.00			
4	Alan Barwick	Personnel	£22,325.00	£803.70	£23,128.70			
5	Mark Hodgson	IT	£16,565.00	£596.34	£17,161.34			
6	Charlie Maverick	IT	£12,525.00	£450.90	£12,975.90			
7	Katy Millford	Personnel	£8,999.00	£323.96	£9,322.96			
8	Luke Moor	Training	£15,525.00	£558.90	£16,083.90			
9	Ann Lynn	Reception	£4,500.00	£162.00	£4,662.00			
10	Caron Hawkeswood	Production	£8,950.00	£322.20	£9,272.20			
11	Helen Martin	Marketing	£6,250.00	£225.00	£6,475.00			
12	Kylie Broadhead	Quality Control	£3,285.00	£118.26	£3,403.26			
13								
14								

Cell references and formulas

This Skill Builder gives practice in using relative and absolute cell references and cell ranges in formulas.

- Basic concepts
- Entering and formatting data
- Basic formulas and functions
- Entering and organising data
- Charts
- Customising worksheets
- Advanced formulas and functions
  - Relative cell addresses
  - Absolute and mixed cell addresses
  - **Exploring different scenarios**
  - **Linking formulas**
  - **Moving cells with formulas**
  - **Inserting cells into formulas**
  - **Deleting cells from formulas**
  - **Cells referenced by formulas**
  - The IF function
  - Exercise on Advanced formulas and functions
- Distributing your worksheets

Skill Builder **2.19**

1 Open the spreadsheet file *kitchen.csv* and calculate the total sales for each of the years (1990, 1995, 2000 and 2004) using a range cell reference.

2 Save the file as *kitchen1.xls*.

3 Calculate the projected sales for each of the years if the company had achieved its aim of 15% increase in sales. You will need to use an absolute cell reference.

4 Format the cells in the *Total* and *Projected* rows as a number to 2 decimal places.

5 Show the formulas in full and produce a printout.

6 Save and close the file.

Your solution should be similar to this

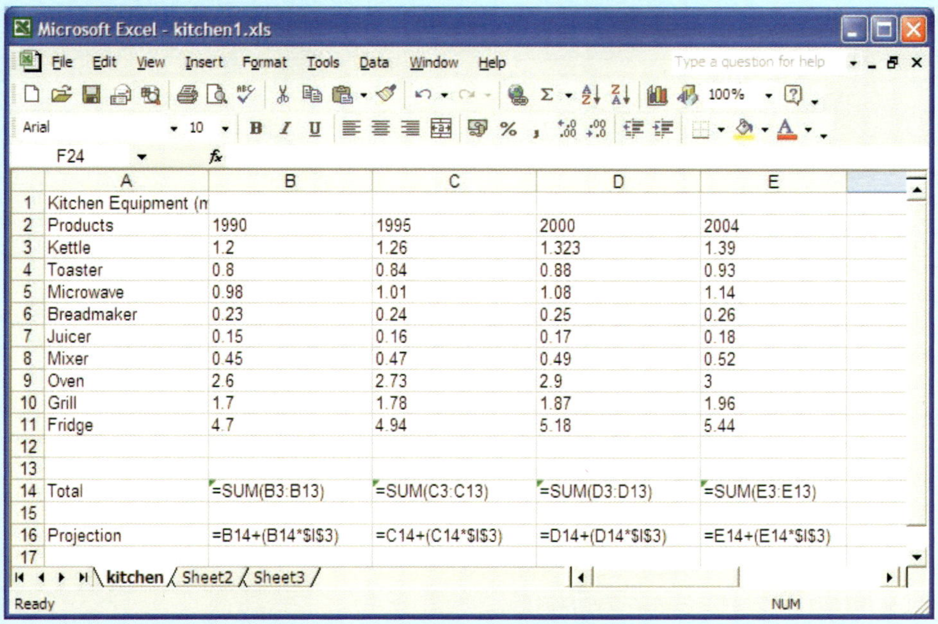

	A	B	C	D	E
1	Kitchen Equipment (n				
2	Products	1990	1995	2000	2004
3	Kettle	1.2	1.26	1.323	1.39
4	Toaster	0.8	0.84	0.88	0.93
5	Microwave	0.98	1.01	1.08	1.14
6	Breadmaker	0.23	0.24	0.25	0.26
7	Juicer	0.15	0.16	0.17	0.18
8	Mixer	0.45	0.47	0.49	0.52
9	Oven	2.6	2.73	2.9	3
10	Grill	1.7	1.78	1.87	1.96
11	Fridge	4.7	4.94	5.18	5.44
12					
13					
14	Total	=SUM(B3:B13)	=SUM(C3:C13)	=SUM(D3:D13)	=SUM(E3:E13)
15					
16	Projection	=B14+(B14*I3)	=C14+(C14*I3)	=D14+(D14*I3)	=E14+(E14*I3)
17					

The IF function

The **IF** function performs a logical test in the spreadsheet and returns one value if the test is true and another value if the test is false.

In addition to the **IF** function, you may be asked to use **SUMIF** or **COUNTIF**.

- Basic concepts
- Entering and formatting data
- Basic formulas and functions
- Entering and organising data
- Charts
- Customising worksheets
- Advanced formulas and functions
  - Relative cell addresses
  - Absolute and mixed cell addresses
  - Exploring different scenarios
  - Linking formulas
  - Moving cells with formulas
  - Inserting cells into formulas
  - Deleting cells from formulas
  - Cells referenced by formulas
  - The IF function
  - Exercise on Advanced formulas and functions
- Distributing your worksheets

Skill Builder 2.20

1 Open the *nursery.xls* spreadsheet and unhide the *Address* and *Age Group* columns.

2 In the Summary Figures section, use a formula containing an appropriate function to show the number of Babies in the *Age Group* column.

3 Produce similar formulas to find the number of 'Toddler' and 'Pre-School' entries.

4 Save the file as *nursery.xls* and close the file.

Your solution should be similar to this

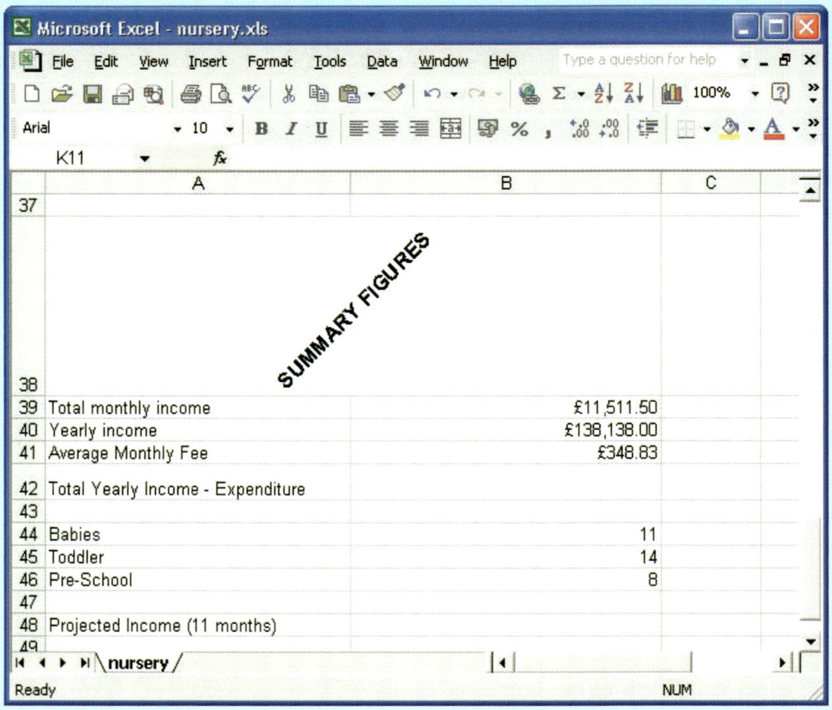

Projected results

In the next Skill Builder you will project the Weekly Income figure if the nursery decided to allow parents four free weeks.

- Basic concepts
- Entering and formatting data
- Basic formulas and functions
- Entering and organising data
- Charts
- Customising worksheets
- Advanced formulas and functions
- Distributing your worksheets

- Relative cell addresses
- Absolute and mixed cell addresses
- Exploring different scenarios
- Linking formulas
- Moving cells with formulas
- Inserting cells into formulas
- Deleting cells from formulas
- Cells referenced by formulas
- The IF function
- **Exercise on Advanced formulas and functions**

Skill Builder **2.21**

1 Open the *nursery.xls* spreadsheet and in the Summary Figures section key in a formula to calculate the *Total Yearly Income - Expenditure* by adding all the *Income after Expenditure* values.

2 In the Fee Structure section of the spreadsheet amend the *Number of months* figure to 11.

3 The *Total Yearly Income - Expenditure* will have changed. Copy this and paste the new value in the *Projected Income* cell.

4 Change the *Number of months* figure back to 12.

Your solution should be similar to this

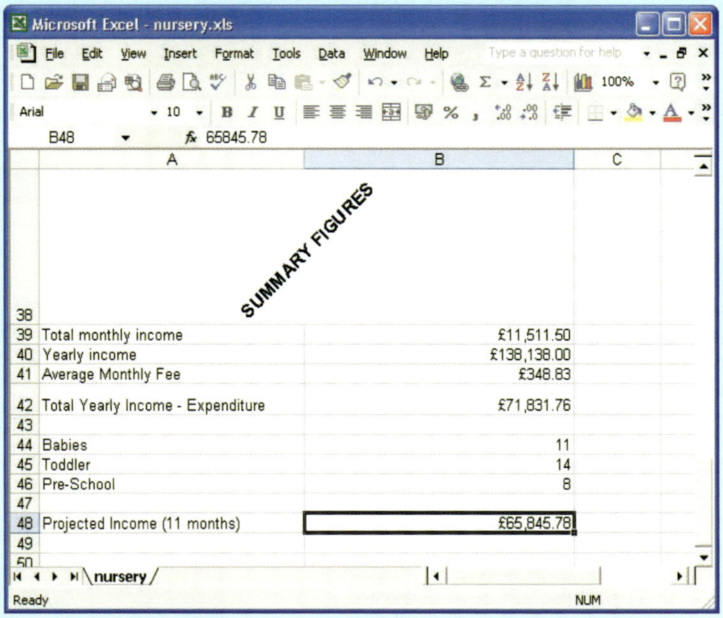

To paste values only: right-click on the target cell, select **Paste special** and select the **Values** radio button.

Mini Assignment 2.4

1 Open the spreadsheet *coursesa.xls*.

2 In the Management Data section use a function to calculate the *Number of IT Courses*.

3 Calculate the *Total Balance* by adding all the values in the *Balance* column.

4 Calculate the *Average Balance*.

5 In the *Increase* column, calculate the value of the increase to be charged. If the *Balance* is less than £20.00, the increase will be the *Balance* value multiplied by the *Increase* percentage. If it is more, then the increase will be 0. You will need to include an absolute cell reference in the formula.

6 Insert a new column heading next to *Increase*, titled *New Course Fee*. Calculate this by adding *Balance* and *Increase*. Replicate for all courses.

7 Insert a new row below *Number of BM courses* in the Management Data section, labelled *Total New Course Fee*. Calculate its value.

8 Change the increase percentage to 10%. Add a new row labelled *Projected Course Fee* under *Total New Course Fee* and show the new projected course fee in this row. Change the increase back to 7.5%.

9 Insert a new row label *Income* in the Management Data Section below the *Projected Course Fee*. Calculate the income by multiplying the *Total Number of Enrolments* from the *projection.csv* file with the *Average Balance* from the *coursesa.xls* spreadsheet. You will need to create a link in your formulas.

10 Save both spreadsheets.

Your solution should be similar to this

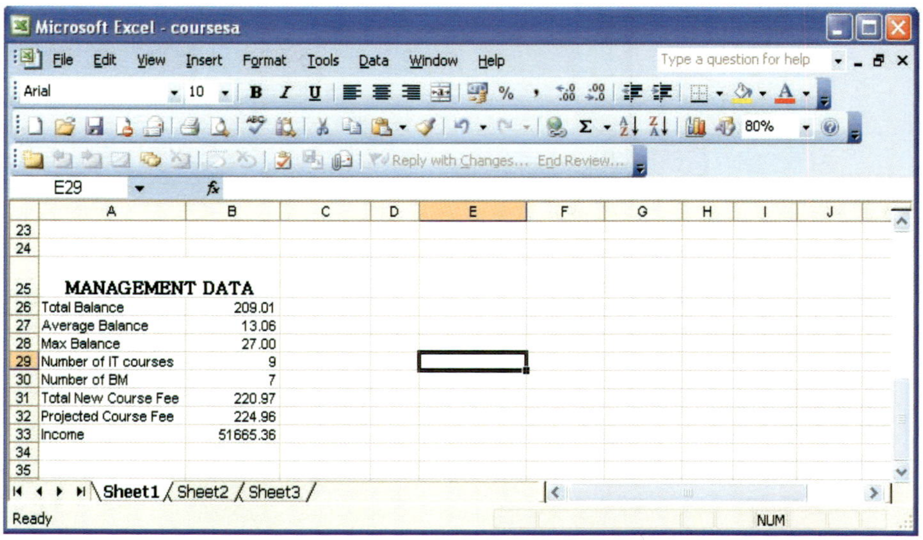

Distributing your worksheets

Page Setup and printing

You will change the Page Setup of the spreadsheet in the following Skill Builder including the page orientation and margins.

- Basic concepts
- Entering and formatting data
- Basic formulas and functions
- Entering and organising data
- Charts
- Customising worksheets
- Advanced formulas and functions
- Distributing your worksheets
  - **Page setup**
  - **Previewing a worksheet**
  - **Printing data**
  - **Printing a chart**
  - Exercise on Distributing your worksheets
  - Task on Distributing your worksheets

Skill Builder **2.22**

1. Open the *nursery.xls* spreadsheet and set the page up as follows:

   Orientation: landscape

   Margins: 2 cm all round
2. Hide the address column and the date registered column.
3. Save the file as *nurseryprn.xls*.
4. Produce a printout. It will need to show all the data fitting on 1 page wide by 2 pages tall.
5. Save and close the file.

Ensure that all data is fully displayed as cells with truncated data (e.g. words not shown in full) are penalised on each occasion.

Units 3 and 11

DATABASES

Databases allow you to store and retrieve information quickly and efficiently using criteria to interrogate the data. You might use a database to hold information about all the learners on a course – their name, date of birth, address and course title. The tutor would be able to interrogate the database and extract data about the age or the results of learners on a particular course.

Data in a database can be held in several tables, related to each other so that data can be extracted from more than one to produce the desired results. In the learners database, you might have one table for the learners' details and another for the course details – and these tables could be linked to produce data relating to any courses. This avoids duplicating data within the database.

- Create, manage and integrate files
- Spreadsheets
- **Databases**
- Presentation graphics
- E-communications

Throughout this unit you will be asked to open files that are supplied in the Resource Bank. They can be found on the Resource Bank CD or in the folder which your tutor may have set up for use with this course.

Getting started

Database concepts

In this first Skill Builder you will open an existing database in Microsoft Access® and use the Office Assistant to find out about database tables.

- Getting started
  - What is a database?
  - Before you begin
  - Launching Microsoft Access
  - The Microsoft Access work area
  - Menu and toolbar basics
  - Using application Help
  - Closing Microsoft Access
  - Exercise on Getting started
- Setting up a database
- Working with tables
- Working with forms
- Sorting records in a database
- Working with queries
- Creating reports and printing

Skill Builder **3.1**

1. Open the database file *practice.mdb*.
2. Use the Office Assistant to find information on tables.
3. Provide a screen print to show you have correctly accessed the information.
4. Close the file.

Your solution should be similar to this

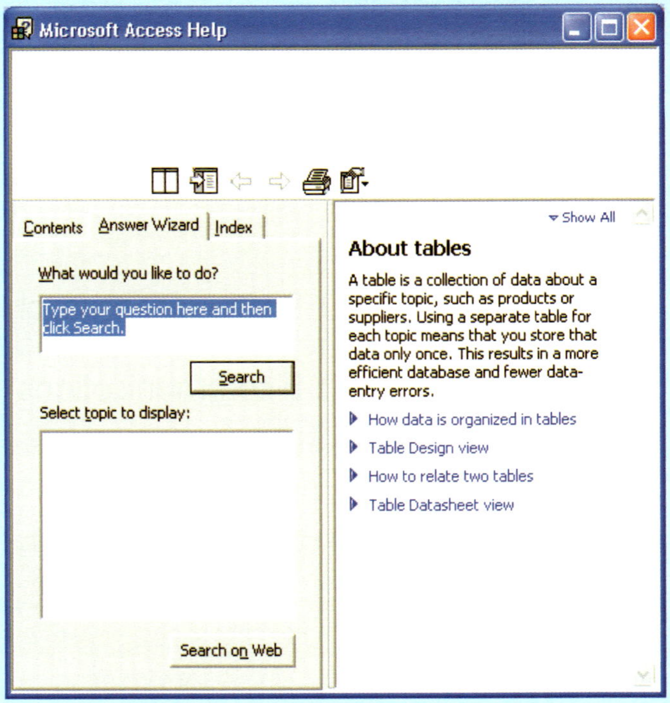

Setting up a database

Creating a new table

In the first part of the CLAIT Plus assessment you will create a new database and enter data from record cards. In the following Skill Builder you will create a new database of tutors.

- Getting started
- Setting up a database
  - **Creating a new table**
  - **Applying data types to fields**
  - **Setting a primary key**
  - Introducing field properties
  - Using validation rules
  - Setting field properties
  - Setting up an index
  - Exercise on Setting up a database
  - Task on Setting up a database
- Working with tables
- Working with forms
- Sorting records in a database
- Working with queries
- Creating reports and printing

Skill Builder **3.2**

1 Load Microsoft Access and create a new database named *tutors*.

2 Click on **Design** to create a new database table in Design view.

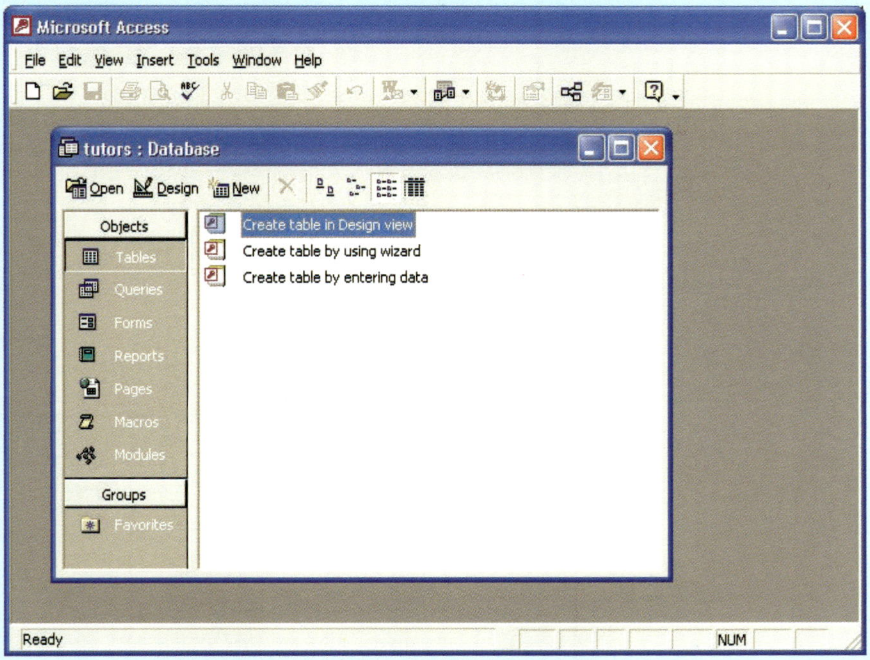

3 Enter these field headings: *Tutor, Learning Centre, Start Date, Course Type, Average Fee, Virtual Course.*

4 Close the table and save as *details*. Do not use a primary key.

Introducing field properties

When you create a database table it is a good idea to set field properties which allow data to be defined in the database. Field properties can help when running queries by searching for dates where the field property is set as date/time.

In the following Skill Builder you will open the *tutors* database and set field properties.

- Getting started
- Setting up a database
  - Creating a new table
  - Applying data types to fields
  - Setting a primary key
  - **Introducing field properties**
  - **Using validation rules**
  - **Setting field properties**
  - **Setting up an index**
  - Exercise on Setting up a database
  - Task on Setting up a database
- Working with tables
- Working with forms
- Sorting records in a database
- Working with queries
- Creating reports and printing

Skill Builder 3.3

1 Open the *tutors* database and access the *details* table in Design view. Your screen should be similar to that shown below.

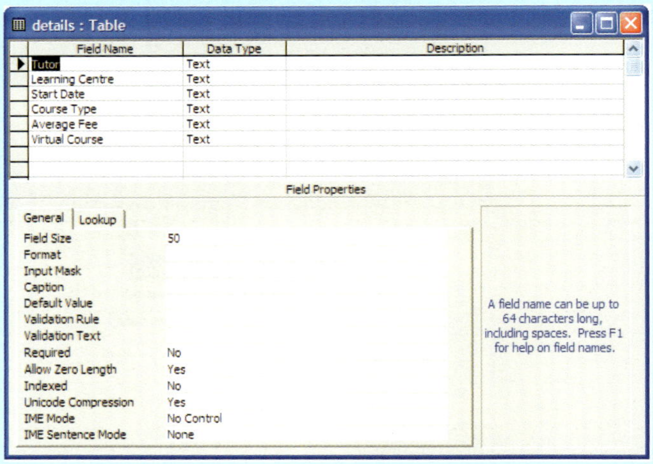

2 Change the data type properties, from the default Text setting, so they are the same as those shown below:

Field	Data Type
Tutor	Text
Learning Centre	Text
Start Date	Date/Time
Course Type	Text
Average Fee	Currency
Virtual Course	Logical Field

3 Close Design view, saving your changes.

Working with tables

Adding data to a table

Once you have created a table and set field properties you are then in a position to key the data directly into the database.

- Getting started
- Setting up a database
- Working with tables
  - Adding data to a table
  - Moving around a table
  - Editing an existing database
  - Modifying a table
  - Exercise on Working with tables
- Working with forms
- Sorting records in a database
- Working with queries
- Creating reports and printing

Skill Builder 3.4

1 Open the *tutors* database and the *details* table. You have been given the following data which is to be entered into the database:

Tutor	Joe Smith	Learning Centre	Barnard Castle Learning Hub
Start Date	01/10/04	Course Type	Information Technology
Average Fee	£15.00	Virtual Course	Yes

Tutor	Andrew White	Learning Centre	Bishopton Learning Hub
Start Date	02/10/04	Course Type	Business and Management
Average Fee	£18.50	Virtual Course	Yes

Tutor	Nicola Johnson	Learning Centre	Gretna Green Learning Hub
Start Date	12/10/04	Course Type	Specialist IT
Average Fee	£21.75	Virtual Course	No

Tutor	Sam Lusty	Learning Centre	Buckingham Learning Hub
Start Date	15/10/04	Course Type	Information Technology
Average Fee	£17.75	Virtual Course	Yes

Tutor	Paul Cartwright	Learning Centre	Penrith Learning Hub
Start Date	01/10/04	Course Type	Information Technology
Average Fee	£15.00	Virtual Course	Yes

Tutor	Ruth Wingate	Learning Centre	Bristol Learning Hub
Start Date	02/10/04	Course Type	Business and Management
Average Fee	£18.50	Virtual Course	Yes

2 The data in the *Course Type* column needs to be encoded as follows:

Information Technology	IT
Business and Management	BM
Specialist IT	SIT

Carry out the amendments using search and replace.

3 Save the table and close the database.

Your database should be similar to this

details : Table

Tutor	Learning Centre	Start Date	Course Type	Average Fee	Virtual Course
Joe Smith	Barnard Castle Learning Hub	01/10/2004	IT	£15.00	☑
Andrew White	Bishopton Learning Hub	02/10/2004	BM	£18.50	☑
Nicola Johnson	Gretna Green Learning Hub	12/10/2004	SIT	£21.75	☐
Sam Lusty	Buckingham Learning Hub	15/10/2004	IT	£17.75	☑
Paul Cartwright	Penrith Learning Hub	01/10/2004	IT	£15.00	☑
Ruth Wingate	Bristol Learning Hub	02/10/2004	BM	£18.50	☑
				£0.00	

Record: 6 of 6

Modifying a table

In the CLAIT Plus assessment you will be required to amend some existing data. In the following Skill Builder you will amend data using the Find and Replace function.

- Getting started
- Setting up a database
- Working with tables
  - Adding data to a table
  - **Moving around a table**
  - **Editing an existing database**
  - **Modifying a table**
  - Exercise on Working with tables
- Working with forms
- Sorting records in a database
- Working with queries
- Creating reports and printing

Skill Builder 3.5

1 Open the *tutors* database and the *details* table.

2 It has been decided not to offer the Specialist IT (SIT) courses so therefore please delete all of these course types from the database.

3 Save and close the file.

Your table should be similar to this

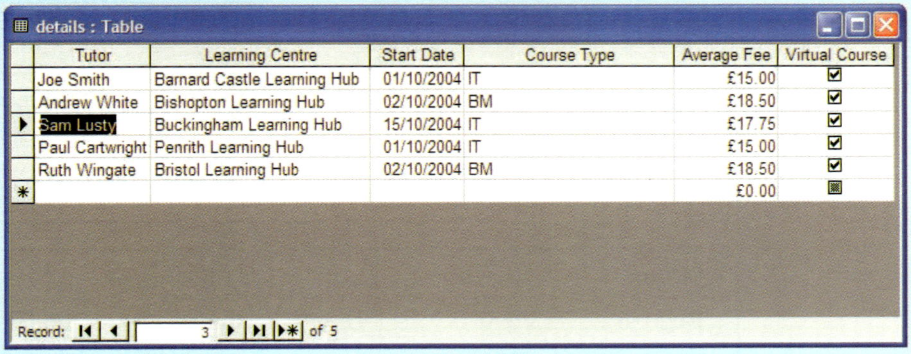

details : Table

Tutor	Learning Centre	Start Date	Course Type	Average Fee	Virtual Course
Joe Smith	Barnard Castle Learning Hub	01/10/2004	IT	£15.00	☑
Andrew White	Bishopton Learning Hub	02/10/2004	BM	£18.50	☑
Sam Lusty	Buckingham Learning Hub	15/10/2004	IT	£17.75	☑
Paul Cartwright	Penrith Learning Hub	01/10/2004	IT	£15.00	☑
Ruth Wingate	Bristol Learning Hub	02/10/2004	BM	£18.50	☑
*				£0.00	

Record: 3 of 5

Mini Assignment 3.1

You are employed as the administrative assistant at Little People Information Centre and have been asked to create a new database to hold the details of Childcare facilities in your local area.

1 Create a new database named *LPeople* and a table named *info*.

2 Enter the following field headings and field types:

Group	Text
Address	Text
Reg No	Text
Category	Text
Date Registered	Date/Time
Average Cost	Currency

3 Key in the data for those childminding facilities that cater for more than 2 children.

4 Encode the data for the category column as below:

Babies	B
Toddler	T
Pre-school	P

Group Barrons			**Address** 6 Derwent Street, Durham		
Reg No LP689		**Date Registered**	05/04/04		
No of Children 3		**Category** Babies		**Average Cost** £17.00	

Group Little Oaks			**Address** 75 High Street, Willington		
Reg No LP690		**Date Registered**	06/03/04		
No of Children 2		**Category** Toddlers		**Average Cost** £15.00	

Group Treasures			**Address** 77 Newgate Street, Crook		
Reg No PP123		**Date Registered**	01/04/04		
No of Children 2		**Category** Babies		**Average Cost** £17.00	

Group 123 Children's Nursery			**Address** Attwood Terrace, Durham		
Reg No PP99		**Date Registered**	12/06/04		
No of Children 23		**Category** Pre-school		**Average Cost** £15.00	

Group Castle View Pre-School		**Address** 4 Commercial Street, Durham	
Reg No LP728	**Date Registered** 19/02/04		
No of Children 47	**Category** Toddler	**Average Cost** £17.00	

Group First Steps		**Address** 166 Fullwell Road, Ryhope	
Reg No PP649	**Date Registered** 09/09/04		
No of Children 15	**Category** Babies	**Average Cost** £21.00	

5 Save and print a copy of the table. Close the database.

Your table should be similar to this

info : Table

Group	Address	Reg No	Category	Date Registered	Average Cost
Barrons	6 Derwent Street, Durham	LP689	B	05/04/2004	£17.00
123 Children's Nursery	Attwood Terrace, Durham	PP99	P	12/06/2004	£15.00
Castle View Pre-School	4 Commercial Street, Durham	LP728	T	19/02/2004	£17.00
First Steps	166 Fullwell Road, Ryhope	PP649	B	09/09/2004	£21.00
					£0.00

Record: 4 of 4

Dates can be used in calculations and are therefore counted as numeric data in the exam. Any date keyed in incorrectly will count as a critical error.

Working with forms

Database forms

In Microsoft Access you can create a form to make it easier to input data than keying it directly into a table.

- Getting started
- Setting up a database
- Working with tables
- Working with forms
  - Introducing database forms
  - Using the Form Wizard to create a form
  - Changing the form design and layout
  - Entering data in a form
  - Using form headers and footers
  - Exercise on Working with forms
- Sorting records in a database
- Working with queries
- Creating reports and printing

Skill Builder 3.6

1 Open the *tutors* database and use the wizard to create a form based on the *details* table.

2 Use all the fields from the table, and select the justified design.

3 Use the standard layout and name the form *tutordetails*.

4 Open the form in Design view and apply bold to the following field headings, *Tutor*, *Start Date*, *Average Fee*.

5 Change the background colour of the form to pale pink.

6 Add your name and centre number in the footer.

7 Save and close the form and database.

Your solution should be similar to this

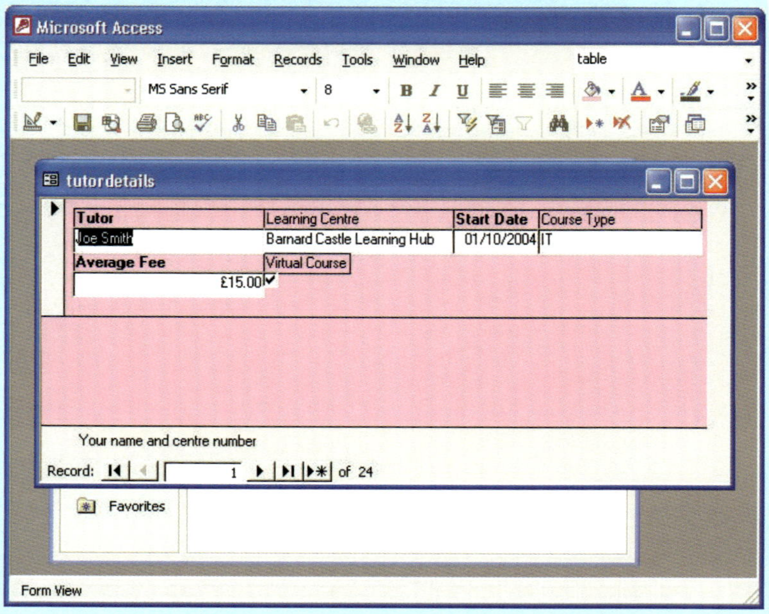

Sorting records in a database

Sorting records in a table

It is sometimes useful to sort data in a database table into a specific order to make it easier to read or locate records. In the following Skill Builder you will sort the records in ascending order of *Average Fee*.

- Getting started
- Setting up a database
- Working with tables
- Working with forms
- Sorting records in a database
  - **Sorting records in a table**
  - Using Filter by Selection
  - Locating data
  - Exercise on Sorting records in a database
  - Task on Sorting records in a database
- Working with queries
- Creating reports and printing

Skill Builder 3.7

1 Open the *tutors* database and the *details* table.

2 Sort the data into ascending order of *Average Fee*.

3 Produce a printout of the database.

4 Save the database and close.

Your screen should be similar to this

details : Table

	Tutor	Learning Centre	Start Date	Course Type	Average Fee	Virtual Course
▶	Joe Smith	Barnard Castle Learning Hub	01/10/2004	IT	£15.00	☑
	Andrew White	Bishopton Learning Hub	01/10/2004	BM	£18.50	☑
	Nicola Johnson	Gretna Green Learning Hub	12/10/2004	SIT	£21.75	☐
	Sam Lusty	Buckingham Learning Hub	15/10/2004	IT	£17.75	☑
	Paul Cartwright	Penrith Learning Hub	01/10/2004	IT	£15.00	☑
	Ruth Wingate	Bristol Learning Hub	02/10/2004	BM	£18.50	☑
*					£0.00	▩

Record: 1 of 6

Locating data

In addition to sorting records in a database you can apply a filter to the database table so that a selection of records matching the filter are shown.

- Getting started
- Setting up a database
- Working with tables
- Working with forms
- Sorting records in a database
  - Sorting records in a table
  - **Using Filter by Selection**
  - **Locating data**
  - Exercise on Sorting records in a database
  - Task on Sorting records in a database
- Working with queries
- Creating reports and printing

Skill Builder 3.8

1 Open the *tutors* database and the *details* table.

2 Click in one of the *Course Type* cells containing 'BM'.

3 Click on the **Filter by Selection** toolbar button.

4 Access should now have filtered all the BM courses and these should be shown.

5 Close the table and file without saving the changes.

Your screen should be similar to this

Filter by Selection

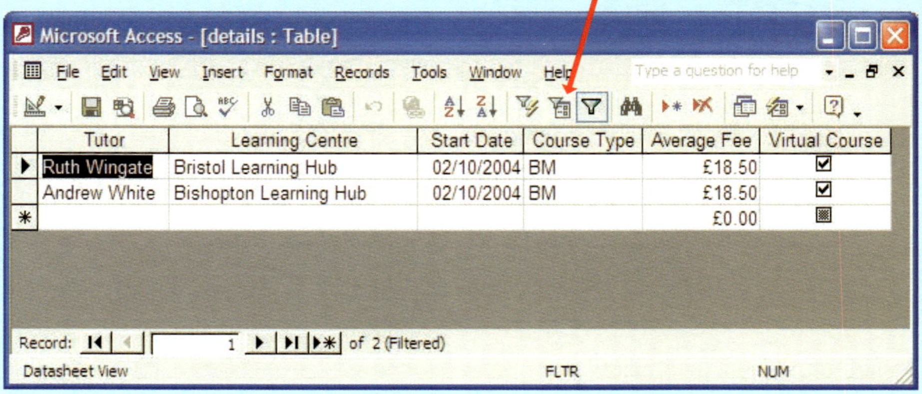

Working with queries

Creating a query

Queries can help you filter data and can help you find data for a specific purpose. In the following Skill Builders you will create different queries to locate specific information from the table you created earlier.

- Getting started
- Setting up a database
- Working with tables
- Working with forms
- Sorting records in a database
- Working with queries
  - **Creating a query**
  - Using criteria in a query
  - Working with operators
  - Changing a query
  - Using wildcards
  - Calculated fields
  - Exercise on Working with queries
  - Task on Working with queries
- Creating reports and printing

Skill Builder 3.9

1. Open the *tutors* database.
2. Create a new query to search for all tutors who teach IT.
3. Enter the criteria IT in the *Course Type* field and run the query (click on the red exclamation mark).
4. Print a copy of the query showing all fields.
5. Close the query and save as *IT*.

Your screen should be similar to this

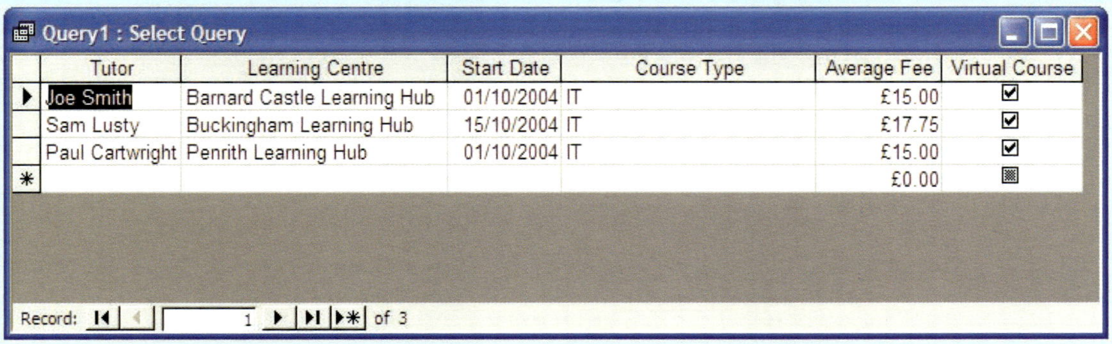

To create a query in Access 2000 select **Queries > New > Design view**
In Access 2002/2003 select **Queries > Create query in Design view**

Working with operators

When you are producing queries and reports you may wish to use operators. In the following Skill Builder you will use the less than '<' operator to find some records from the database table.

- Getting started
- Setting up a database
- Working with tables
- Working with forms
- Sorting records in a database
- Working with queries
  - Creating a query
  - **Using criteria in a query**
  - **Working with operators**
  - Changing a query
  - Using wildcards
  - Calculated fields
  - Exercise on Working with queries
  - Task on Working with queries
- Creating reports and printing

Skill Builder **3.10**

1 Using the *tutors* database, create another query which searches for Virtual Courses where the *Average Fee* is less than £17.00.

2 Show the following fields ONLY in the order given:

Tutor

Average Fee

Virtual Course

Learning Centre

3 Run the query, close and save as *Virtual*.

Your screen should be similar to this

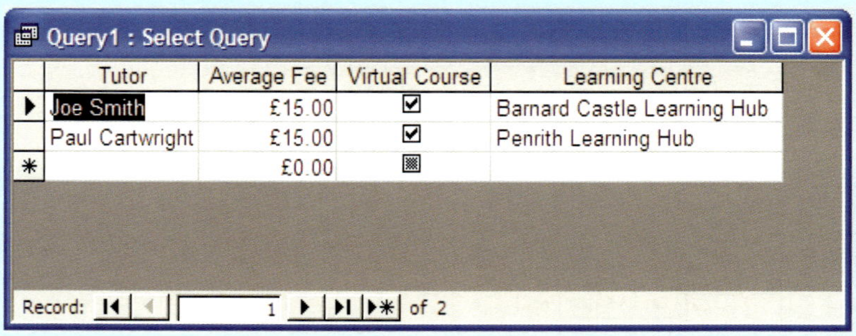
Query1 : Select Query

Tutor	Average Fee	Virtual Course	Learning Centre
Joe Smith	£15.00	☑	Barnard Castle Learning Hub
Paul Cartwright	£15.00	☑	Penrith Learning Hub
	£0.00		

Record: 1 of 2

Using wildcards

Wildcards can help you find data where you want to look for multiple data or where you are unsure of the data you are searching for.

- Getting started
- Setting up a database
- Working with tables
- Working with forms
- Sorting records in a database
- Working with queries
  - Creating a query
  - Using criteria in a query
  - Working with operators
  - **Changing a query**
  - **Using wildcards**
  - Calculated fields
  - Exercise on Working with queries
  - Task on Working with queries
- Creating reports and printing

A wildcard is a special character that can stand for any other character(s) in searches, where you want to find records with similar data. For example, '*' stands for any one or more characters, so if you want to search for all customers whose surname begins with W you can do this by setting W* as the criterion.

Skill Builder **3.11**

1. Open the *tutors* database (if not already open).
2. Create a new query to search for all learning centres that begin with the letter B and where the start date is between 1st and 10th October.
3. Run the query and produce a printout. Save the query as *Bhubs* and close the file.

Your screen should be similar to this

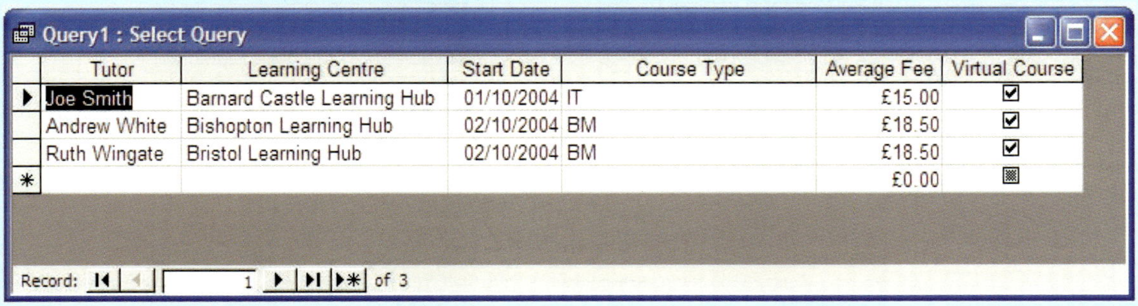

Calculated fields

You can also create queries which include calculations and in the following Skill Builder you will create a new field in the query and calculate a 15% pay increase for the tutors.

- Getting started
- Setting up a database
- Working with tables
- Working with forms
- Sorting records in a database
- Working with queries
  - Creating a query
  - Using criteria in a query
  - Working with operators
  - Changing a query
  - Using wildcards
  - **Calculated fields**
  - Exercise on Working with queries
  - Task on Working with queries
- Creating reports and printing

Skill Builder 3.12

1 Open the *tutors* database (if not already open).

2 Create a new query to calculate the *Average Fee* if the tutors were to receive a 15% pay rise (i.e. * 1.15).

3 Create a new query in Design view. Use the **Expression Builder** to calculate the pay increase.

4 Name the new field *Increase Fee* and format it as currency.

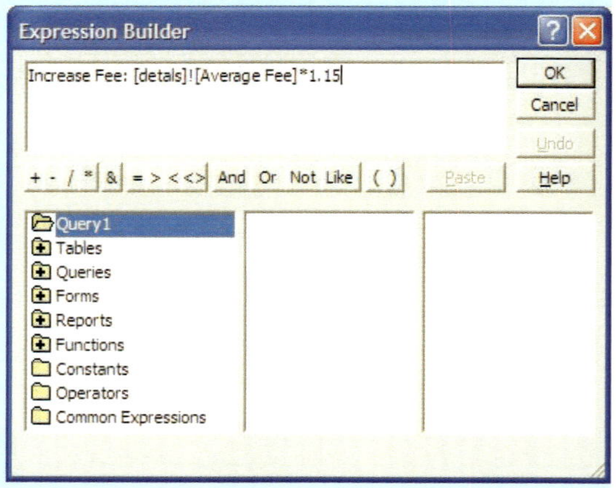

5 Show all the fields in the query. Run the query, print one copy and save it as *Increase*.

6 Close the file.

Your screen should be similar to this

Query1 : Select Query

Tutor	Learning Centre	Start Date	Course Type	Average Fee	Increase Fee
Joe Smith	Barnard Castle Learning Hub	01/10/2004	IT	£15.00	£17.25
Andrew White	Bishopton Learning Hub	01/10/2004	BM	£18.50	£21.28
Nicola Johnson	Gretna Green Learning Hub	12/10/2004	SIT	£21.75	£25.01
Sam Lusty	Buckingham Learning Hub	15/10/2004	IT	£17.75	£20.41
Paul Cartwright	Penrith Learning Hub	01/10/2004	IT	£15.00	£17.25
Ruth Wingate	Bristol Learning Hub	02/10/2004	BM	£18.50	£21.28
*				£0.00	

Record: 1 of 6

Creating reports and printing

Creating a report from a query

You can produce different reports, e.g. tabular, column or grouped. This Skill Builder gives you practice in producing a column report. It is based on the query you created before which looked for the IT courses.

- Getting started
- Setting up a database
- Working with tables
- Working with forms
- Sorting records in a database
- Working with queries
- Creating reports and printing
  - **Creating a basic report**
  - **Formatting a report**
  - **Creating a report from a query**
  - Making changes to a report
  - Introduction to printing
  - Printing database objects
  - Creating and printing labels
  - Importing data from other applications
  - Exercise on Creating reports and printing
  - Task on Creating reports and printing

Skill Builder **3.13**

1 Open the *tutors* database and create a report based on the *IT* query.

To create a column report: Select **Reports > Create Reports by using a Wizard**.

2 Title the report *IT Tutors*.

3 Produce a column report showing the following fields: *Tutor*, *Learning Centre*, *Start Date*.

4 Sort the *Start Date* into ascending order.

5 Save the report as *IT Tutors* and close.

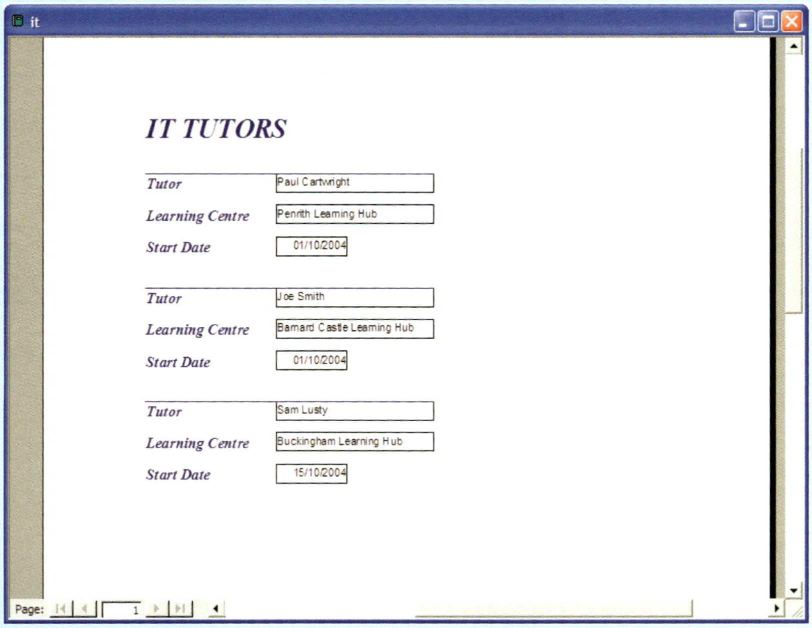

Making changes to a report

Once you have created a report you will need to check that all data is displayed as requested and shown in full. You can change the font, font sizes and add headers/footers to your report.

- Getting started
- Setting up a database
- Working with tables
- Working with forms
- Sorting records in a database
- Working with queries
- Creating reports and printing
  - Creating a basic report
  - Formatting a report
  - Creating a report from a query
  - **Making changes to a report**
  - Introduction to printing
  - Printing database objects
  - Creating and printing labels
  - Importing data from other applications
  - Exercise on Creating reports and printing
  - Task on Creating reports and printing

Skill Builder 3.14

1. Open the *tutors* database.
2. Locate the text file *tutors.csv*. Copy and paste the data, or import the file into the *details* table of the *tutors* database.
3. Create a grouped report using the Virtual Query titled:

   Virtual Courses on Offer
4. The report should be grouped by the *Tutor* field.
5. Display these field headings: *Tutor*, *Average Fee*, *Learning Centre*.
6. Sort into ascending order of *Average Fee*.
7. Display the Total of the *Average Fee* on the report.
8. Print the report in portrait ensuring that all data is displayed on one A4 page.
9. Save the report as *Courses* and close the report.

Your solution should be like this

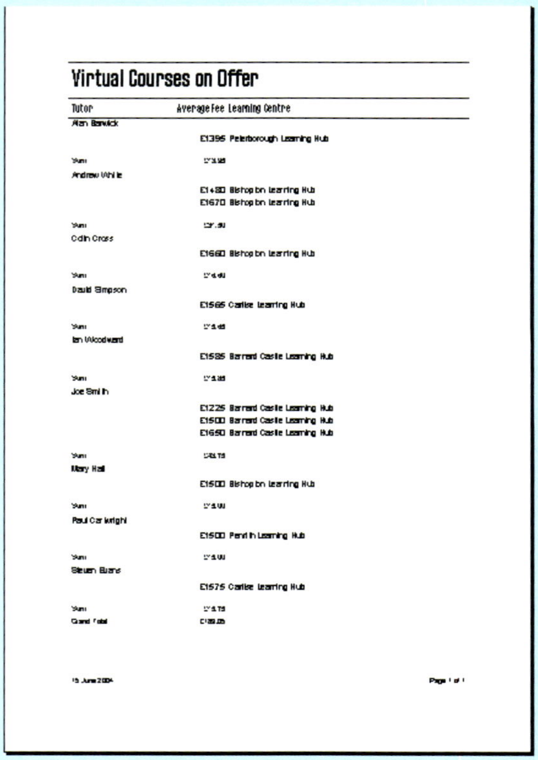

Virtual Courses on Offer

Tutor	Average Fee	Learning Centre
Alan Barwick		
	£1395	Peterborough Learning Hub
Sum	[illegible]	
Andrew White		
	£1480	Bishopton Learning Hub
	£1670	Bishopton Learning Hub
Sum	[illegible]	
Colin Cross		
	£1660	Bishopton Learning Hub
Sum	[illegible]	
David Simpson		
	£1565	Carlisle Learning Hub
Sum	[illegible]	
Ian Woodward		
	£1585	Barnard Castle Learning Hub
Sum	[illegible]	
Joe Smith		
	£1225	Barnard Castle Learning Hub
	£1500	Barnard Castle Learning Hub
	£1650	Barnard Castle Learning Hub
Sum	[illegible]	
Mary Hall		
	£1500	Bishopton Learning Hub
Sum	[illegible]	
Paul Cartwright		
	£1500	Penrith Learning Hub
Sum	[illegible]	
Steven Evans		
	£1575	Carlisle Learning Hub
Sum	[illegible]	
Grand Total	[illegible]	

15 June 2004 Page 1 of 1

Introduction to printing

You can print selected items rather than whole reports and/or tables.

- Getting started
- Setting up a database
- Working with tables
- Working with forms
- Sorting records in a database
- Working with queries
- Creating reports and printing
  - Creating a basic report
  - Formatting a report
  - Creating a report from a query
  - Making changes to a report
  - **Introduction to printing**
  - **Printing database objects**
  - Creating and printing labels
  - Importing data from other applications
  - Exercise on Creating reports and printing
  - Task on Creating reports and printing

Skill Builder **3.15**

1. Open the *tutors* database and open the *IT Tutors* report.
2. You will notice that this report is displayed on two pages.
3. Open the **Print** dialogue box and print one copy of the first page of the report only.
4. Close the report.
5. Open the *details* table and select the first six records.
6. Open the **Print** dialogue box and print 2 copies of these selected records.
7. Close the table.
8. Close the database.

Creating and printing labels

Remember that labels can be printed on plain paper and need not be printed on proper label paper.

- Getting started
- Setting up a database
- Working with tables
- Working with forms
- Sorting records in a database
- Working with queries
- Creating reports and printing
  - Creating a basic report
  - Formatting a report
  - Creating a report from a query
  - Making changes to a report
  - Introduction to printing
  - Printing database objects
  - Creating and printing labels
  - Importing data from other applications
  - Exercise on Creating reports and printing
  - Task on Creating reports and printing

Skill Builder 3.16

1 Using the *tutors* database, produce a set of labels from the *details* table and display the following fields:

Tutor *Learning Centre*
Start Date

2 Use the command **Reports > New > Label Wizard** and select the table details.

3 The following dialogue box is shown – select the size of label that you are going to print out on and click **Next**.

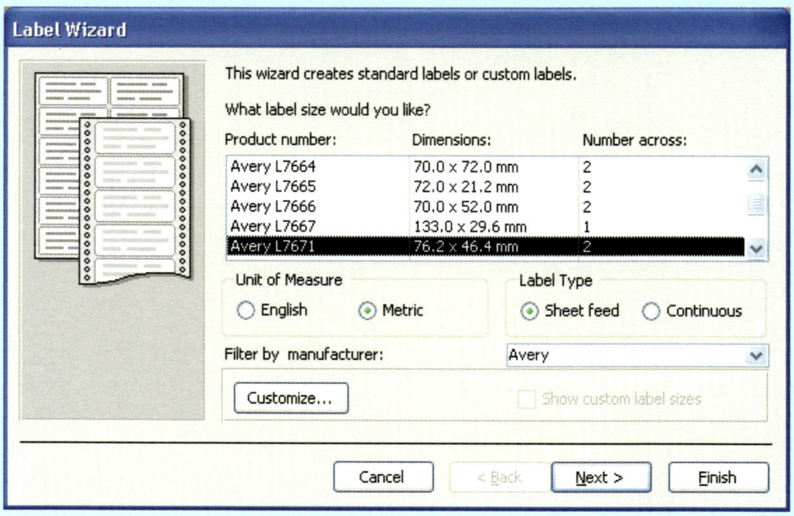

4 Select the font and size to be displayed.

5 Select the required fields (*Tutor*, *Learning Centre*, *Start Date*) from the **Available Fields:** box.

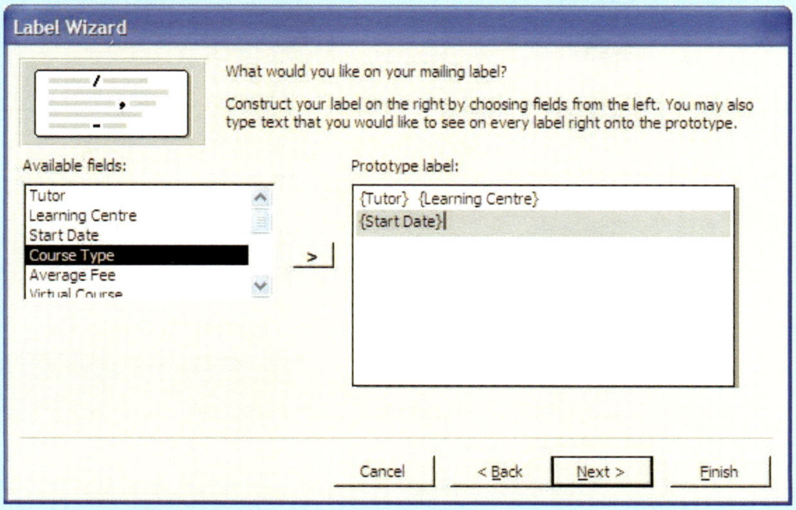

6 Select **Next** and **Finish**.

7 Save the report as *labels* and close the report.

Mini Assignment 3.2

1 Open the database *Lpeople*.

2 Import the data from the *Lpeople.csv* file.

3 Create the labels for the Administration Staff from the updated database.

Display these fields: *Group*, *Address*, *Category*.

Do not display field names on the labels.

Order the labels in ascending order of *Category*.

Use a label size that will allow the labels to be printed on two pages.

Insert your name and centre number in the footer.

Your labels should look like this

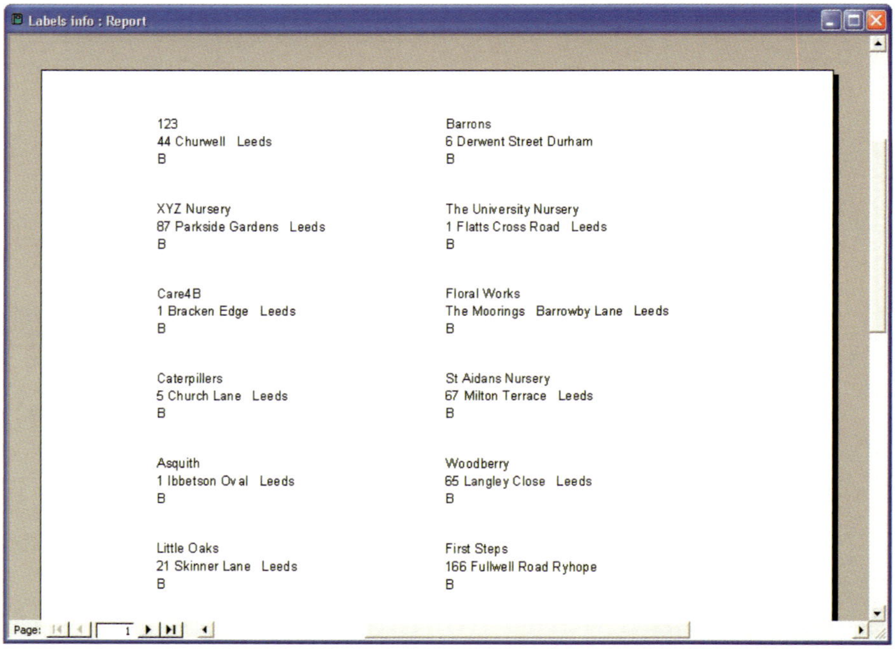

4 In a query find only the *Babies* and *Toddler* groups. Create a new field called *Admin* and calculate the Admin by adding the fee of 3.75 to the *Average Cost*. Save the query as *Admin*.

5 Using the *Admin* query saved in step 4 produce a grouped report titled:

Average Cost

Group the report by *Category*.

Display the *Category*, *Group*, *Address*, *Date Registered*, *Average Cost*, *Admin* fields in this order.

Sort on the *Date Registered* field in ascending order.

Display the average of the *Admin Fee*.

Display the average summary with the £ sign to 2 decimal places.

Change the *Avg* label to read *Average Admin Fee*.

Centre the data in the *Group* and *Address* columns.

Use an automatic field to display the date and the page numbers. Enter your name and centre number as a footer. Save and print the report in portrait orientation to fit on one page.

Your report should look like this

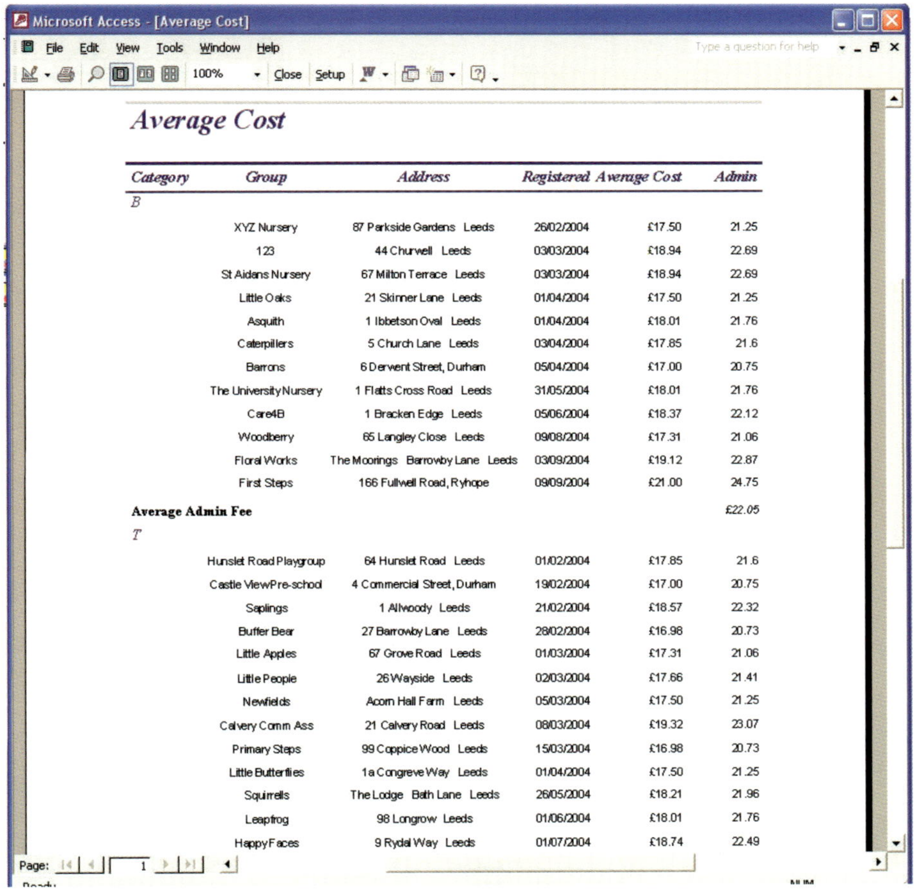

Average Cost

Category	*Group*	*Address*	*Registered*	*Average Cost*	*Admin*
B					
	XYZ Nursery	87 Parkside Gardens Leeds	26/02/2004	£17.50	21.25
	123	44 Churwell Leeds	03/03/2004	£18.94	22.69
	St Aidans Nursery	67 Milton Terrace Leeds	03/03/2004	£18.94	22.69
	Little Oaks	21 Skinner Lane Leeds	01/04/2004	£17.50	21.25
	Asquith	1 Ibbetson Oval Leeds	01/04/2004	£18.01	21.76
	Caterpillers	5 Church Lane Leeds	03/04/2004	£17.85	21.6
	Barrons	6 Derwent Street, Durham	05/04/2004	£17.00	20.75
	The University Nursery	1 Flatts Cross Road Leeds	31/05/2004	£18.01	21.76
	Care4B	1 Bracken Edge Leeds	05/06/2004	£18.37	22.12
	Woodberry	65 Langley Close Leeds	09/08/2004	£17.31	21.06
	Floral Works	The Moorings Barrowby Lane Leeds	03/09/2004	£19.12	22.87
	First Steps	166 Fullwell Road, Ryhope	09/09/2004	£21.00	24.75
Average Admin Fee					*£22.05*
T					
	Hunslet Road Playgroup	64 Hunslet Road Leeds	01/02/2004	£17.85	21.6
	Castle View Pre-school	4 Commercial Street, Durham	19/02/2004	£17.00	20.75
	Saplings	1 Allwoody Leeds	21/02/2004	£18.57	22.32
	Buffer Bear	27 Barrowby Lane Leeds	28/02/2004	£16.98	20.73
	Little Apples	67 Grove Road Leeds	01/03/2004	£17.31	21.06
	Little People	26 Wayside Leeds	02/03/2004	£17.66	21.41
	Newfields	Acorn Hall Farm Leeds	05/03/2004	£17.50	21.25
	Calvery Comm Ass	21 Calvery Road Leeds	08/03/2004	£19.32	23.07
	Primary Steps	99 Coppice Wood Leeds	15/03/2004	£16.98	20.73
	Little Butterflies	1a Congreve Way Leeds	01/04/2004	£17.50	21.25
	Squirrels	The Lodge Bath Lane Leeds	26/05/2004	£18.21	21.96
	Leapfrog	98 Longrow Leeds	01/06/2004	£18.01	21.76
	Happy Faces	9 Rydal Way Leeds	01/07/2004	£18.74	22.49

6 The Information Centre wants to find out which Nurseries are based in Durham. In a query find only the nurseries whose address is in Durham and who have been registered between April and September 2004.

7 Save the query as *Durham*.

8 Using the *Durham* query saved at step 6 produce a tabular report titled:

Nurseries in Durham

Display these fields in the following order: *Group*, *Category*, *Reg No*, *Date Registered*.

Sort the data into ascending order of *Category* and then into ascending order of *Reg No*.

Insert your name, date and page number and centre number.

Save and print the report to fit on one page in portrait orientation.

Your report should look like this

Nurseries in Durham

Group	Category	Reg No	Date Registered
Barrons	B	LP689	05/04/2004
Just Learning	P	LP695	01/04/2004
123 Children's Nursery	P	PP99	12/06/2004

9 Create a new query where the address is not Durham and the category of children catered for is Babies or Toddlers only.

10 Produce a columnar report titled Nurseries outside Durham.

Use the *Group*, *Address* and *Category* fields.

Sort into ascending order on the *Group* field.

Add your name and centre number to the footer. Do not show the date.

Save and print the report to fit two pages in portrait orientation.

Close the database.

Your report should look like this

Nurseries outside Durham

Group	123
Address	44 Churwell Leeds
Category	B
Group	Asquith
Address	1 Ibbetson Oval Leeds
Category	B
Group	Buffer Bear
Address	27 Barrowby Lane Leeds
Category	T
Group	Calvery Comm Ass
Address	21 Calvery Road Leeds
Category	T
Group	Care4B
Address	1 Bracken Edge Leeds
Category	B
Group	Caterpillers
Address	5 Church Lane Leeds
Category	B
Group	First Steps
Address	166 Fullwell Road, Ryhope
Category	B
Group	Floral Works
Address	The Moorings Barrowby L
Category	B
Group	Happy Faces
Address	9 Rydal Way Leeds
Category	T
Group	Hunslet Road Playgroup
Address	64 Hunslet Road Leeds
Category	T
Group	Leapfrog
Address	98 Longrow Leeds
Category	T
Group	Little Angels
Address	64 Bath Lane Leeds
Category	T

31 August2004 Page 1 of 2

Units 5 and 13

PRESENTATION GRAPHICS

Microsoft PowerPoint® is an application program which you can use to create a presentation. This can be displayed on screen, or projected onto a whiteboard allowing all the delegates in a room to view it.

The presentation can be printed out showing the slides in full, and you can add your own notes which can also be printed to help you give your presentation.

PowerPoint presentations can be animated and timings applied, so that they can run automatically, for example in a reception area to give details of a new product.

- Create, manage and integrate files
- Spreadsheets
- Databases
- Presentation graphics
- E-communications

Throughout this chapter you will be asked to open files that are supplied in the Resource Bank. They can be found on the Resource Bank CD or in the folder which your tutor may have set up for use with this course.

Getting started

The PowerPoint screen and tools

- Getting started
- Creating text slides
- Changing the look of slides
- Preparing on-screen presentations
- Charts
- Graphics
- Preparing and publishing presentations

- About presentations
- Introducing the PowerPoint work area
- Menu and toolbar basics
- Working with multiple presentations
- Saving presentations
- Using application Help
- Closing the presentation and application
- Exercise on Getting started

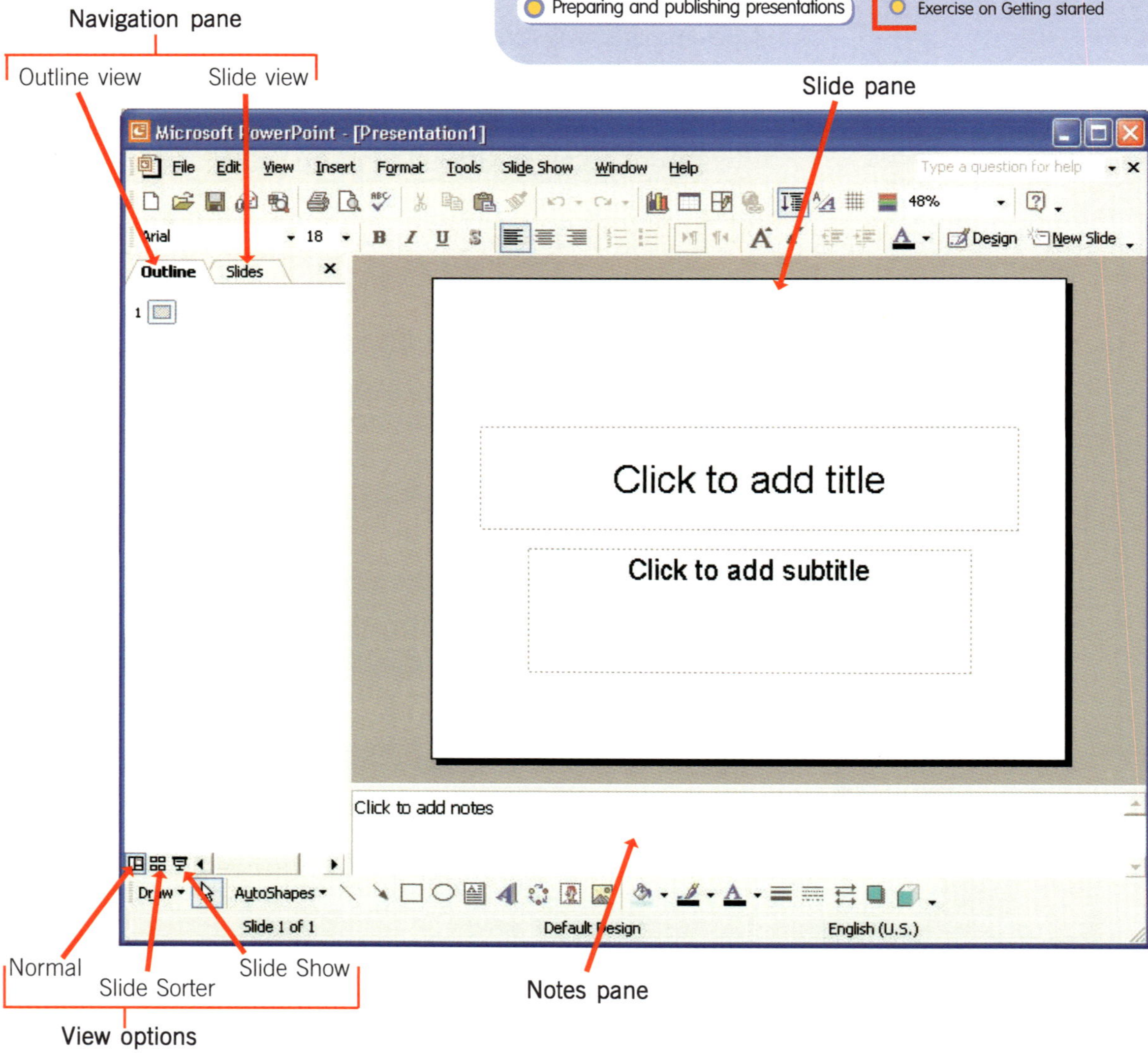

This screen shot is from PowerPoint 2002. The 2000 version has a slightly different collection of tools, and **Outline view** is selected from the **View** options, rather than being an alternative to the Slide view in the navigation pane.

Starting a new presentation

In CLAIT Plus the presentation text has been prepared for you and you are required to copy the text from a text file onto the appropriate slides of a presentation.

You will create a new presentation relating to the history of famous teddy bears.

Skill Builder **5.1**

1 Open the supplied file *bears.txt*. Create a title slide in PowerPoint and copy the text as indicated in the text file onto the slide.

2 Save the presentation as *bears.ppt*.

Your slide should look like this

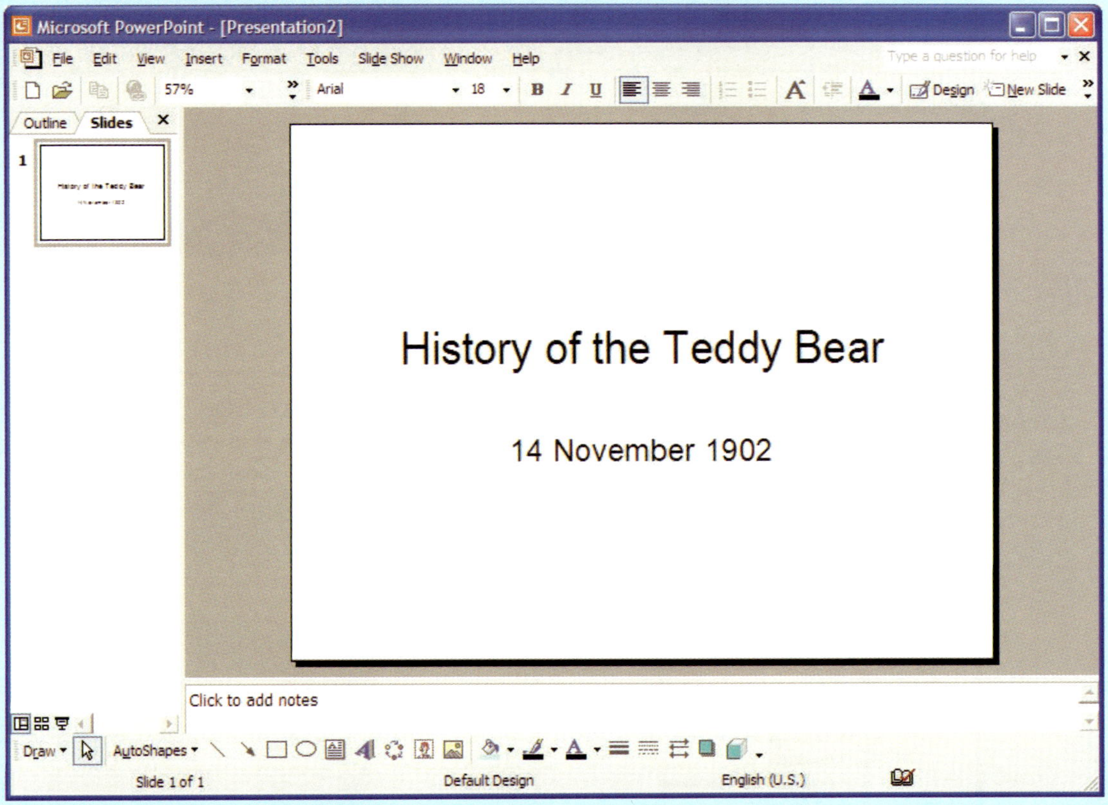

Creating text slides

Moving and duplicating text

Now that you have created a title slide you will create two more Title and Text slides and add more text. You will also move and copy text within the presentation.

- Getting started
- Creating text slides
  - Working with placeholders
  - Moving and duplicating text
  - Changing alignment and line spacing
  - Using bulleted and numbered lists
  - Working with indents and tabs
  - Duplicating data between presentations
  - Working in Outline view
  - Exercise on Creating text slides
  - Task on Creating text slides
- Changing the look of slides
- Preparing on-screen presentations
- Charts
- Graphics
- Preparing and publishing presentations

Skill Builder **5.2**

1. Open the presentation *bears.ppt* and create two new Title and Text slides.
2. Copy the text from the *bears.txt* file onto the two slides you have created.
3. Move the bullets, ‘Bear in the Big Bear House’ and ‘Barnaby Bear’ from slide 2 to become the last two bullets on slide 3.
4. Save the file as *bears.ppt* and close the file.

Your solution should be similar to this

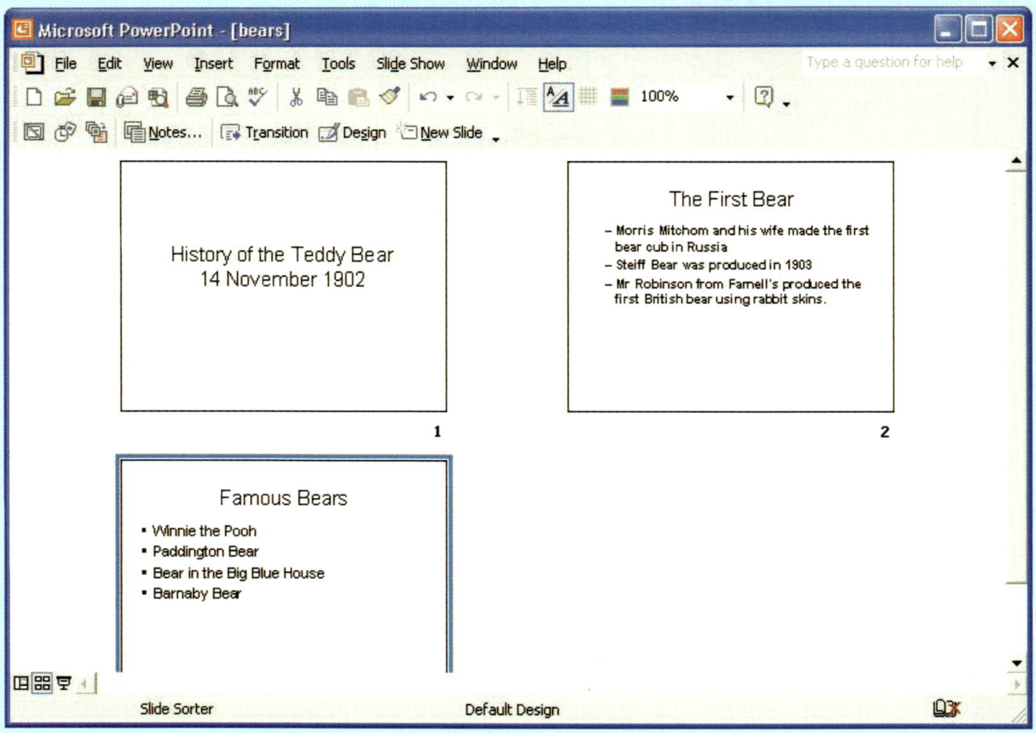

Working in Outline view

Outline view is an area where you can create the text of presentations, edit the content of slides or move bullets or slides more easily.

- Getting started
- Creating text slides
  - Working with placeholders
  - Moving and duplicating text
  - Changing alignment and line spacing
  - Using bulleted and numbered lists
  - Working with indents and tabs
  - Duplicating data between presentations
  - Working in Outline view
  - Exercise on Creating text slides
  - Task on Creating text slides
- Changing the look of slides
- Preparing on-screen presentations
- Charts
- Graphics
- Preparing and publishing presentations

Skill Builder **5.3**

1 Create a new presentation and key in the following text on three slides:

Slide 1 Outline View

Slide 2 Toolbar

- View
- Outlining
- Toolbars

Slide 3 The End

2 Highlight the text on slide 2 and move bullet 2, 'Outlining' to be the last item.

3 Add a new slide 3 titled: **A new slide**.

4 Switch to Outline View. Save the file as *outline.ppt* and close the file.

Your solution should be similar to this

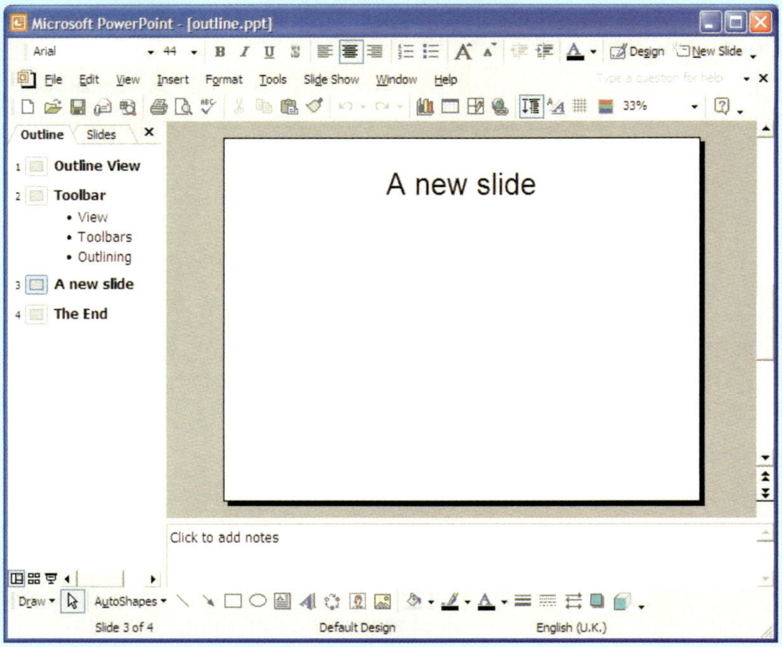

Changing the look of slides

Design templates

Design templates allow you to apply a design to one or all templates in a presentation. These templates have predefined background colours and images, and font styles, sizes, colours and other formatting.

- Getting started
- Creating text slides
- Changing the look of slides
  - Formatting text
  - Working with design templates
  - Working with master slides
  - Adding headers and footers to slides
  - Adding borders and shading to a placeholder
  - Exercise on Changing the look of slides
  - Task on Changing the look of slides
- Preparing on-screen presentations
- Charts
- Graphics
- Preparing and publishing presentations

Skill Builder 5.4

1 Open the presentation *outline.ppt* and apply a colourful design (e.g. *Proposal)* to all slides.

2 Click on the **Slide Sorter** view to see that the colours on the slide have changed but the text remains the same.

3 Save the file as *outline1.ppt* and close the file.

Your solution should be similar to this

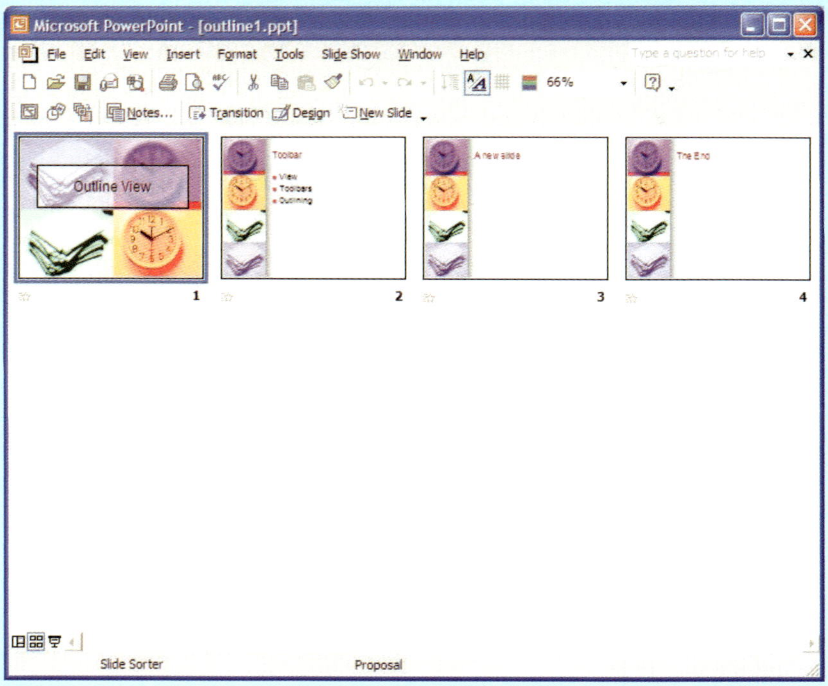

Office 2000 – to access the templates, select **Format > Apply Design Template...**
Office 2002/2003 – select **Format > Slide design...**

Working with master slides

The master slide allows you to set formatting instructions and headers/footers which are applied to all the slides in the presentation.

The house style of a presentation can be applied using the master slide.

- Getting started
- Creating text slides
- Changing the look of slides
  - Formatting text
  - Working with design templates
  - **Working with master slides**
  - Adding headers and footers to slides
  - Adding borders and shading to a placeholder
  - Exercise on Changing the look of slides
  - Task on Changing the look of slides
- Preparing on-screen presentations
- Charts
- Graphics
- Preparing and publishing presentations

Skill Builder **5.5**

1. Open the presentation *bears.ppt.*
2. View the master slide by selecting **View > Master > Slide Master**.
3. Apply a sans serif font, 36 pt, bold, italics and centre alignment to the master title style.
4. Apply a serif font, 32 pt, left aligned to the first bullet style on the master slide.
5. Close the master view and ensure that the new styles have been applied across all slides.
6. Once you are happy both styles have been applied consistently, save the file as *bears.ppt* and close the file.

Your solution should be similar to this

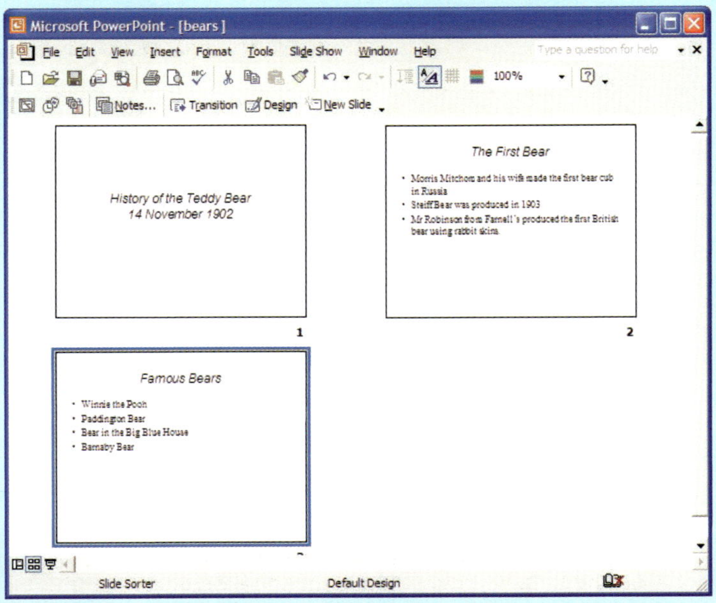

Adding headers and footers to slides

In the following Skill Builder you will add headers and footers to the master slide.

- Getting started
- Creating text slides
- Changing the look of slides
- Preparing on-screen presentations
- Charts
- Graphics
- Preparing and publishing presentations

- Formatting text
- Working with design templates
- Working with master slides
- **Adding headers and footers to slides**
- Adding borders and shading to a placeholder
- Exercise on Changing the look of slides
- Task on Changing the look of slides

Skill Builder 5.6

1 Open the file *bears.ppt* and view the master slide. Insert the date and slide numbers as a footer on all slides.

2 Draw a text box in the top left corner of the master slide and add the text History of Bears as a header on all slides.

3 Close the master slide and ensure that all headers/footers are shown on each slide.

4 Save the file as *bears.ppt* and close the file.

Your solution should be similar to this

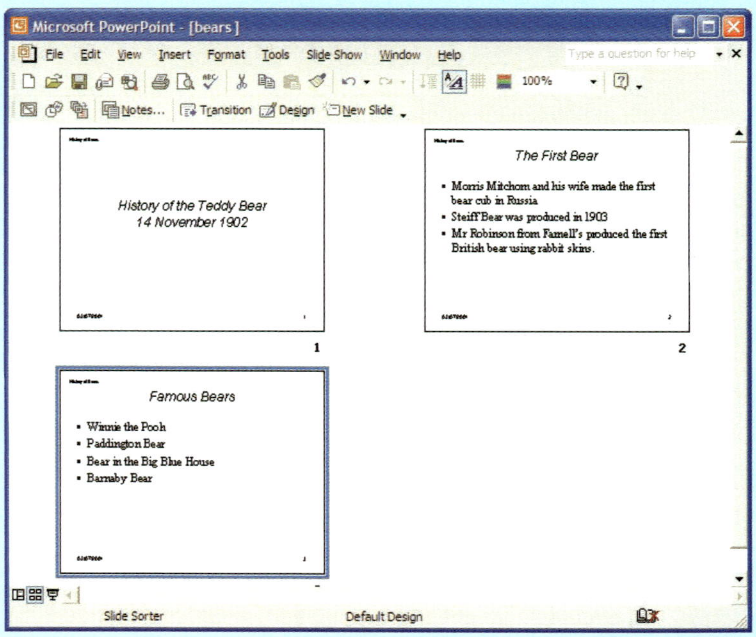

Take care as PowerPoint XP sometimes resizes title fonts automatically to get them to fit into the placeholders. This would be penalised as an accuracy error.

Adding borders and shading to a placeholder

You can apply a border to placeholders to enhance the presentation when displayed and printed.

- Getting started
- Creating text slides
- Changing the look of slides
  - Formatting text
  - Working with design templates
  - Working with master slides
  - Adding headers and footers to slides
  - **Adding borders and shading to a placeholder**
  - Exercise on Changing the look of slides
  - Task on Changing the look of slides
- Preparing on-screen presentations
- Charts
- Graphics
- Preparing and publishing presentations

Skill Builder **5.7**

1 Open the file *bears.ppt* and view the master slide.

2 Add a border around the 'Click to edit Master title style' placeholder. Select **Format > Placeholder** and the following dialogue box appears.

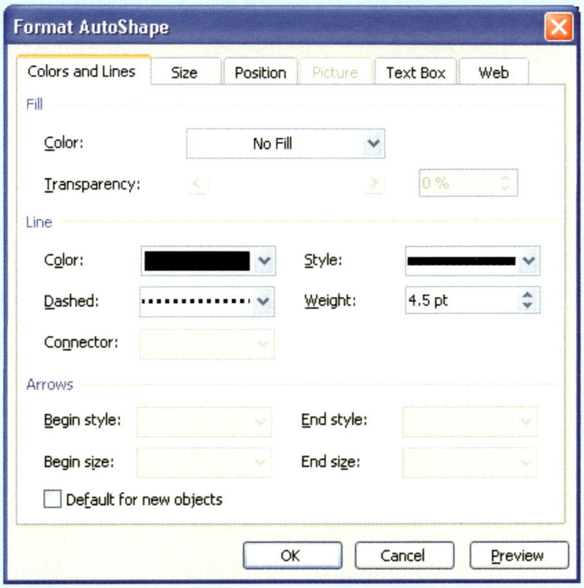

3 Set the border to be a dotted line with a weight of 4.5 pt.

4 Close the master slide and ensure that the border is shown around all titles.

5 Save the file as *bears.ppt* and close the file.

Mini Assignment 5.1

You are working for NYTravel and have been asked to create a presentation advertising New York City as a popular holiday destination. The presentation will be shown in various advertising outlets.

You will need access to the *newyork.txt* file.

1 Create a new presentation.

2 Open the text file *Newyork* and copy the prepared text onto the slides as indicated in the text file.

3 Create a master slide and apply the following house styles:

Master slide

Feature	Colour/Effect	Font size	Position	Additional information
Background	any	–	–	1 background only (can be white) Ensure that text is clearly legible
Text	–	10 pt	top left	Your name and centre number
Slide number	–	–	bottom right	
Date	–	–	bottom centre	UK format (day, month, year) Use an automatic field

Text

Style name	Font	Font size	Style	Alignment
Heading	Serif	50 pt	bold	centre
Bullet	Serif	30 pt	to include a bullet character	left
Sub-bullet	Sans serif	25 pt	italic and with a bullet	left
Speaker's notes	Sans serif	20 pt	–	left

4 Ensure that the house style and master slide text has been applied consistently throughout the presentation.

5 Save the presentation as *newyork.ppt* and close the file.

Your solution should be similar to this

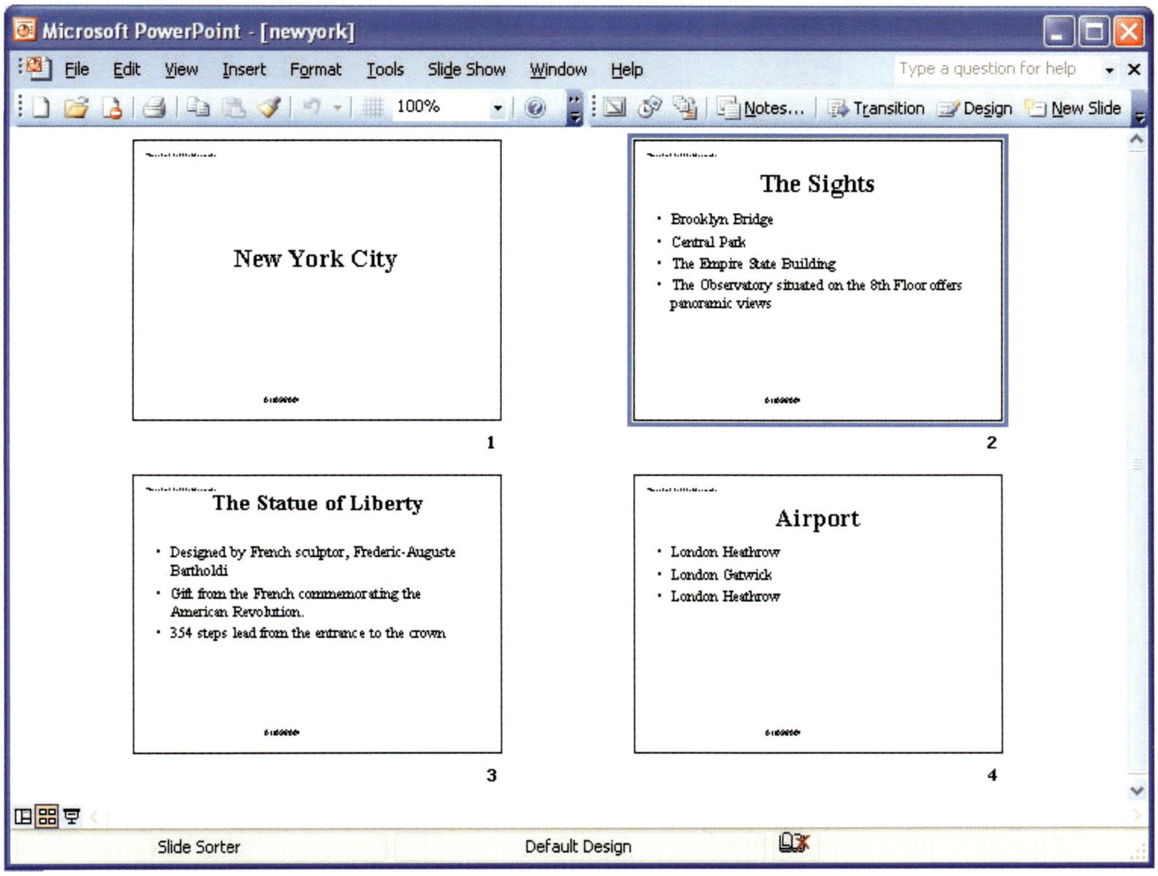

Preparing on-screen presentations

Animations and transitions

In the CLAIT Plus assessment you will be asked to apply builds and transitions. A build is an animation in PowerPoint that controls the way that text and images appear on the screen. Transitions are visual effects and introduce the slides in an on-screen slide show.

- Getting started
- Creating text slides
- Changing the look of slides
- Preparing on-screen presentations
  - Working in Slide Sorter View
  - Animations and transitions
  - Custom animations
  - Running a slide show on screen
  - Setting timings for your slides
  - Linking slides
  - Exercise on Preparing on-screen presentations
- Charts
- Graphics
- Preparing and publishing presentations

Skill Builder 5.8

1 Open the file *bears.ppt*.

2 Change to Slide Sorter view so that you can see a copy of the slides and the animations and transitions.

3 Apply the **Dissolve** animation to each slide.

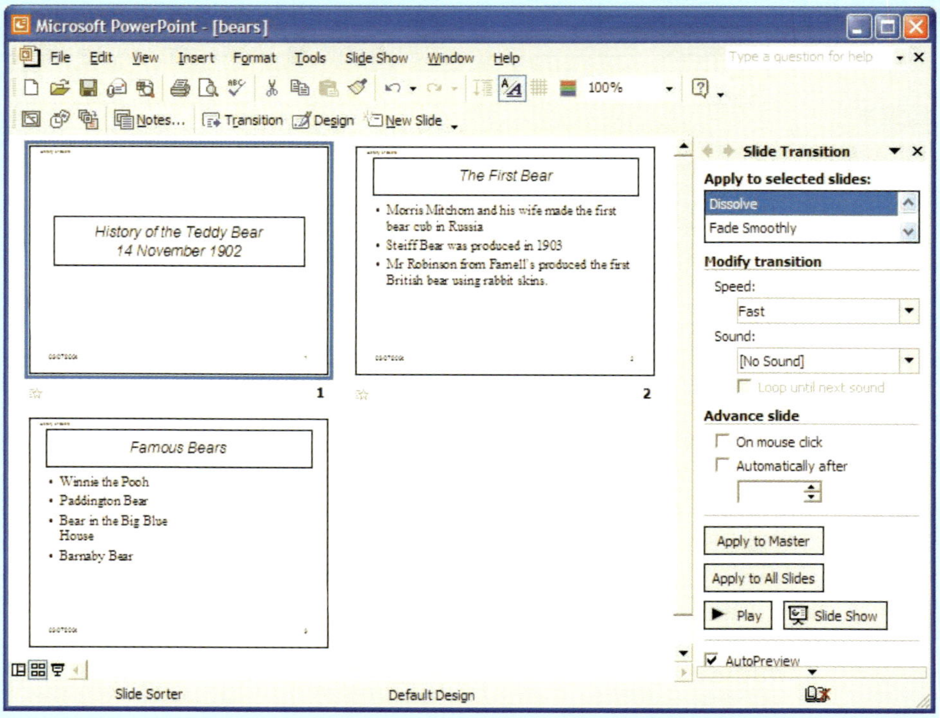

Select **Slide Show > Preview Animation** to check that the animations you have set are working as you want them to.

In PowerPoint XP the way that builds and transition effects are added is different and the screen print will be different – in XP a star shows the transitions.

4 Apply the **Fade in one by one** transition to all of the slides.

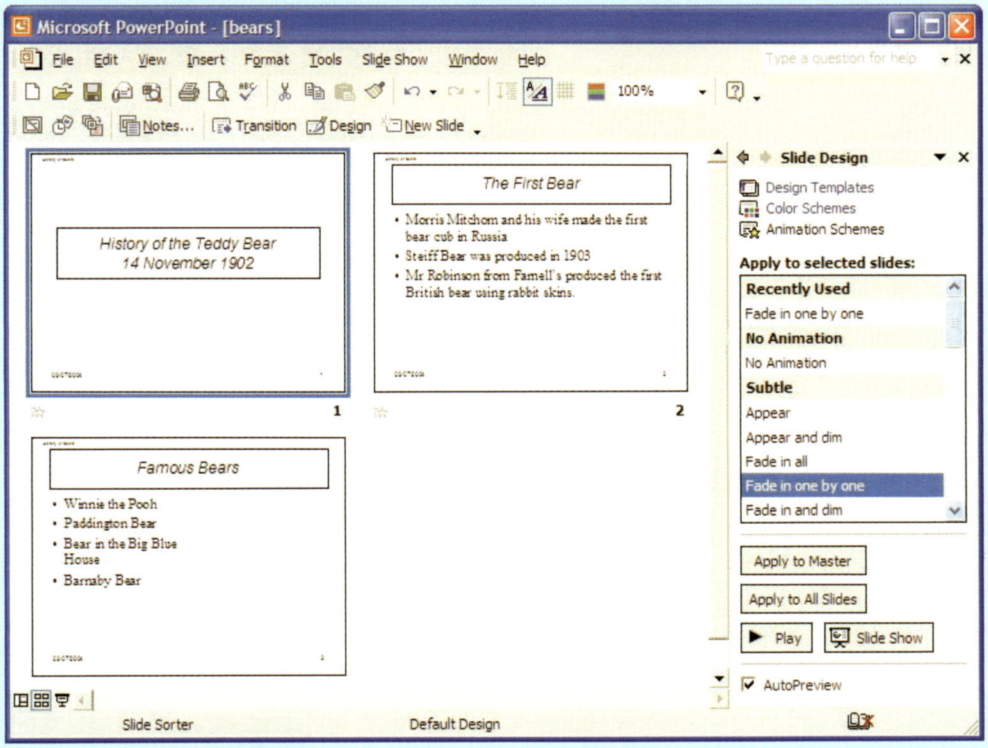

5 Check that the transitions and animations have been applied to all slides by running a slide show.

6 Save the file as *bears.ppt* and close the file.

In the exam, if you use PowerPoint XP, you will need to produce two screen prints – one to show the transition that has been added and one to show the animations that have been added.

Running a slide show

Set up a slide show so that it can be browsed at a kiosk full screen without any operator assistance.

- Getting started
- Creating text slides
- Changing the look of slides
- Preparing on-screen presentations
  - Working in Slide Sorter View
  - Animations and transitions
  - **Custom animations**
  - **Running a slide show on screen**
  - Setting timings for your slides
  - Linking slides
  - Exercise on Preparing on-screen presentations
- Charts
- Graphics
- Preparing and publishing presentations

Skill Builder **5.9**

1. Open the *bears.ppt* file.
2. Set up a slide show so that it can be browsed at a kiosk using a full screen. Select **Slide Show > Set Up Show** to open the dialogue box.

Use the kiosk option for a full screen presentation

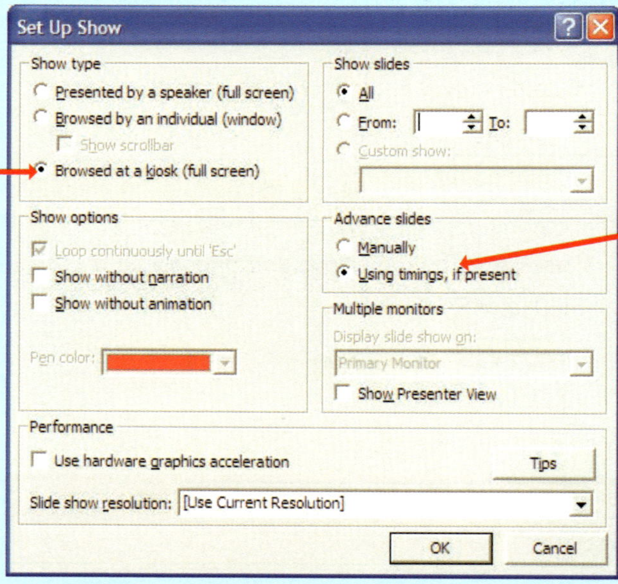

Select **Using timings** for an automatic presentation

3. Ensure that slide 1 is selected so that the slide show begins at the first slide.
4. Use your mouse to move between the slides ensuring that all slides are shown.
5. Save the file as *bears.ppt* and close the file.

Timings

In this Skill Builder you will add timings to your presentation so that it can be run automatically, allowing sufficient time for each slide to be shown.

- Getting started
- Creating text slides
- Changing the look of slides
- Preparing on-screen presentations
  - Working in Slide Sorter View
  - Animations and transitions
  - Custom animations
  - Running a slide show on screen
  - **Setting timings for your slides**
  - Linking slides
  - Exercise on Preparing on-screen presentations
- Charts
- Graphics
- Preparing and publishing presentations

Skill Builder **5.10**

1 Open the file *bears.ppt* and add a blank final slide.

2 Apply timings as given below. Use **Slide Show > Slide Transition**.

Slide 1 – 10 seconds

Slide 2 – 20 seconds

Slide 3 – 20 seconds

Slide 4 – 40 seconds

3 Check that all timings have been applied correctly and run the slide show. Produce a screen print to show that the timings have been correctly applied.

4 Save the file as *bears.ppt* and close the file.

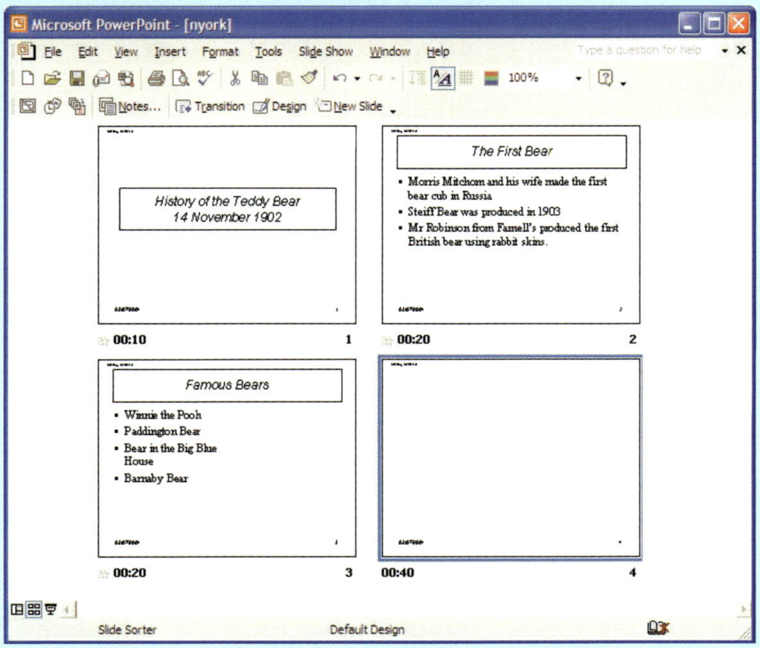

Linking slides

In PowerPoint you can link slides by creating a hyperlink from one to another. This allows you, when viewing the presentation, to go to another slide quickly.

You can insert a hyperlink on selected text, or add one using an action button.

- Getting started
- Creating text slides
- Changing the look of slides
- Preparing on-screen presentations
  - Working in Slide Sorter View
  - Animations and transitions
  - Custom animations
  - Running a slide show on screen
  - Setting timings for your slides
  - **Linking slides**
  - Exercise on Preparing on-screen presentations
- Charts
- Graphics
- Preparing and publishing presentations

Skill Builder **5.11**

1. Open the presentation *bears.ppt* and create a new slide 4 before the final blank slide at the end of the presentation.
2. Key in the title Sales Projections.
3. Go back to Slide 3. On the **Draw** toolbar, select **AutoShapes** then **Action Buttons**. Pick one like this and drag to draw it in the bottom right-hand corner of the slide.

4. The **Action Settings** dialogue box will open. Select *Next Slide* to link to.

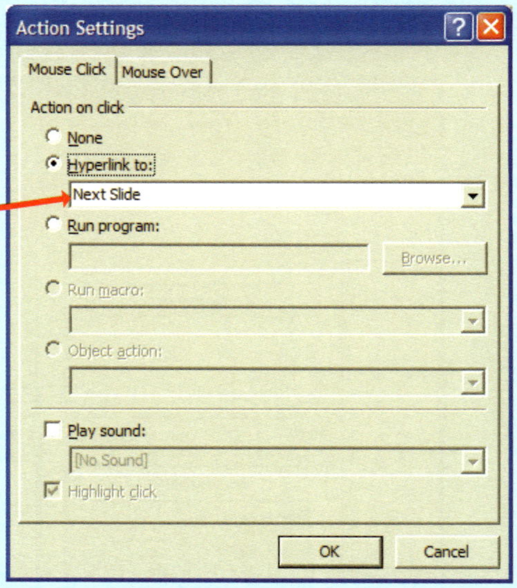

Link to the next slide

5. Check that the link works by running the slide show and clicking on the action button.
6. Save the file as *bears.ppt* and close the file.

Hide a slide

Sometimes you might not want all of your audience to see all of your presentation and in this case you may wish to hide a slide.

Hidden slides are shown in Slide Sorter view with a box that has a line through the slide number. In the exam you will need to produce a screen print to show evidence of the hidden slide.

Skill Builder 5.12

1. Open the presentation *bears.ppt* and hide slide 4.
2. To hide slide 4 – right-click on it in the Slide Sorter screen, and select **Hide Slide**.
3. Run a slide show and check that the slide has been hidden.
4. Save the file as *bears.ppt* and close the file.

In the exam, failure to insert a hyperlink to access hidden slides is penalised as a critical error.

Charts

Creating organisation charts

In the following Skill Builder you will create an organisation chart for the bears presentation.

Getting started
Creating text slides
Changing the look of slides
Preparing on-screen presentations
Charts
Graphics
Preparing and publishing presentations

Creating organisation charts
Making changes to organisation charts
Introducing data charts
Working with data charts
Changing the look of data charts
Inserting a table
Exercise on Charts
Task on Charts

Skill Builder **5.13**

1 Open the presentation *bears.ppt* and create a new slide 5.

2 Create a new slide and select Title or Diagram and Organization slide. Enter the title A Family Business.

3 Key in the chart as shown below.

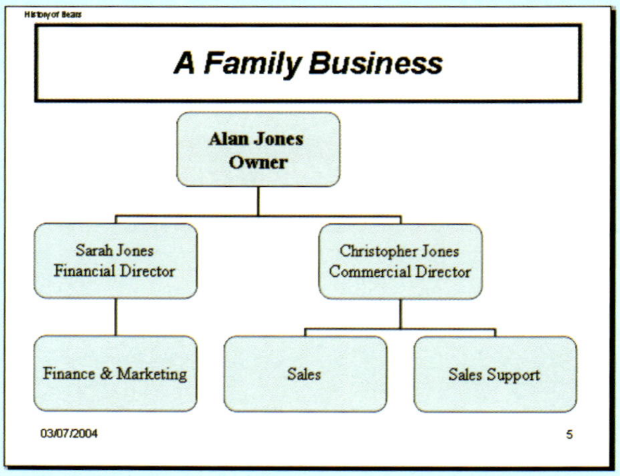

4 Apply the following house style to the organisation chart:

Feature	Font	Font size	Style
Top level	Serif	24 pt	bold
Assistant/subordinates	Serif	20 pt	-

5 Save the presentation as *bears.ppt* and close the file.

In PowerPoint XP, you cannot add co-workers at top level. But you could draw your own box – the rounded rectangle in the Flowcharts Autoshape set looks just the same – and add your own lines and text using the Draw tools.

Introducing data charts

In this Skill Builder you will create a bar chart to show the sales the company has achieved over the last four years and the projected sales for the coming 12 months with the information that has been provided by the Finance Division of the company.

- Getting started
- Creating text slides
- Changing the look of slides
- Preparing on-screen presentations
- Charts
  - Creating organisation charts
  - Making changes to organisation charts
  - **Introducing data charts**
  - **Working with data charts**
  - **Changing the look of data charts**
  - Inserting a table
  - Exercise on Charts
  - Task on Charts
- Graphics
- Preparing and publishing presentations

Skill Builder **5.14**

1 Open the presentation *bears.ppt* and using the following information create on Slide 4 a bar chart titled Sales Projections.

	Winnie the Pooh	Paddington	Barnaby Bear
2002	20.4	27.4	16.5
2003	30.6	24.9	34.6
2004	68.9	49.3	45.0

Your chart should look similar to this

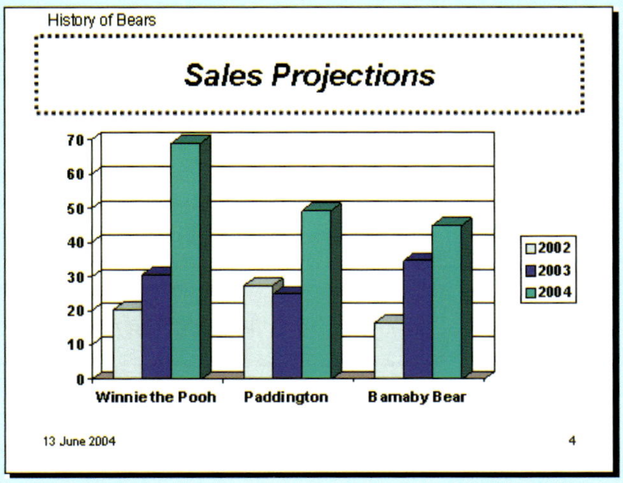

2 Format the chart as per the house style sheet given below:

Style Name	Font	Font size	Style
Labels/legend	Sans serif	14 pt	bold

3 Save the presentation as *bears.ppt* and close the file.

Inserting a table

In this Skill Builder you will create a table using existing data that we have already been provided with in the presentation.

- Getting started
- Creating text slides
- Changing the look of slides
- Preparing on-screen presentations
- Charts
  - Creating organisation charts
  - Making changes to organisation charts
  - Introducing data charts
  - Working with data charts
  - Changing the look of data charts
  - **Inserting a table**
  - Exercise on Charts
  - Task on Charts
- Graphics
- Preparing and publishing presentations

Skill Builder **5.15**

1. Open the presentation *bears.ppt* and create a new slide 5 as a title and table slide. Add the new title Market Share.
2. Apply the text and key in the additional data as shown below:

Bear	First Sold	Percentage of Market
Winnie the Pooh	1929	42%
Paddington	1958	38%
Barnaby Bear	2002	20%

3. Format the table according to the house style sheet.

Style Name	Font	Font size	Style	Alignment
Text	Sans serif	20 pt	no bullet characters	left
Number	Sans serif	20 pt	no bullet characters	right

4. Save the presentation as *bears.ppt* and close the file.

Your solution should be similar to this

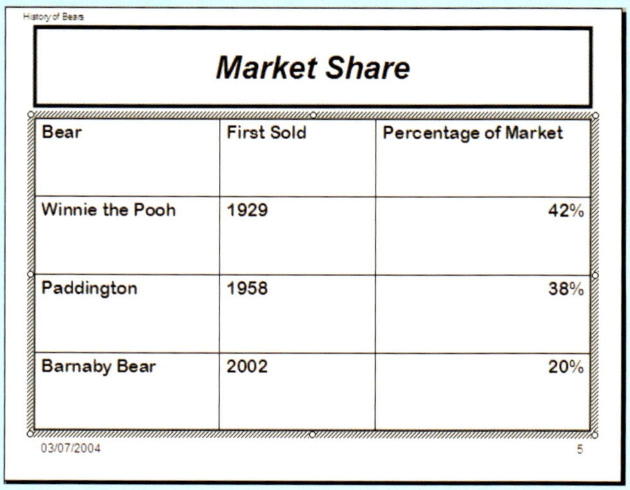

Mini Assignment 5.2

1 Open the presentation *newyork.ppt* and apply two different transitions to each of the slides in the presentation.

2 Apply two different build effects to each of the slides in the presentation.

3 Apply the following timings:

Slide 1	10 seconds
Slide 2	20 seconds
Slide 3	20 seconds
Slide 4	20 seconds

4 Save the presentation as *newyork1.ppt*.

5 Before slide 4, insert a new slide – which becomes the new number 4 – and key in the organisation chart below:

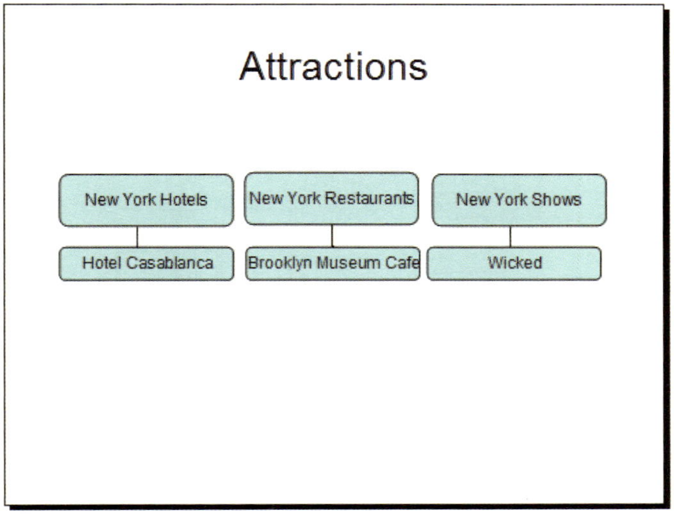

6 Create a new slide numbered 5 with the title **Sales**, and use this data to create a bar chart on it:

Number of visitors

2001	26.58
2002	30.20
2003	31.71

7 Amend slide 6 and apply a table layout using the information provided below:

Airport	**Airline**	**Average Price**
London Heathrow	Web Special	£240
London Gatwick	UK Airways	£369
London Heathrow	USA Airways	£398

8 Create a link on slide 4 (organization slide) to slide 5 (chart slide).

9 Hide the chart slide.

10 Save the presentation *newyork1.ppt* and close the file.

Your solution should be similar to this

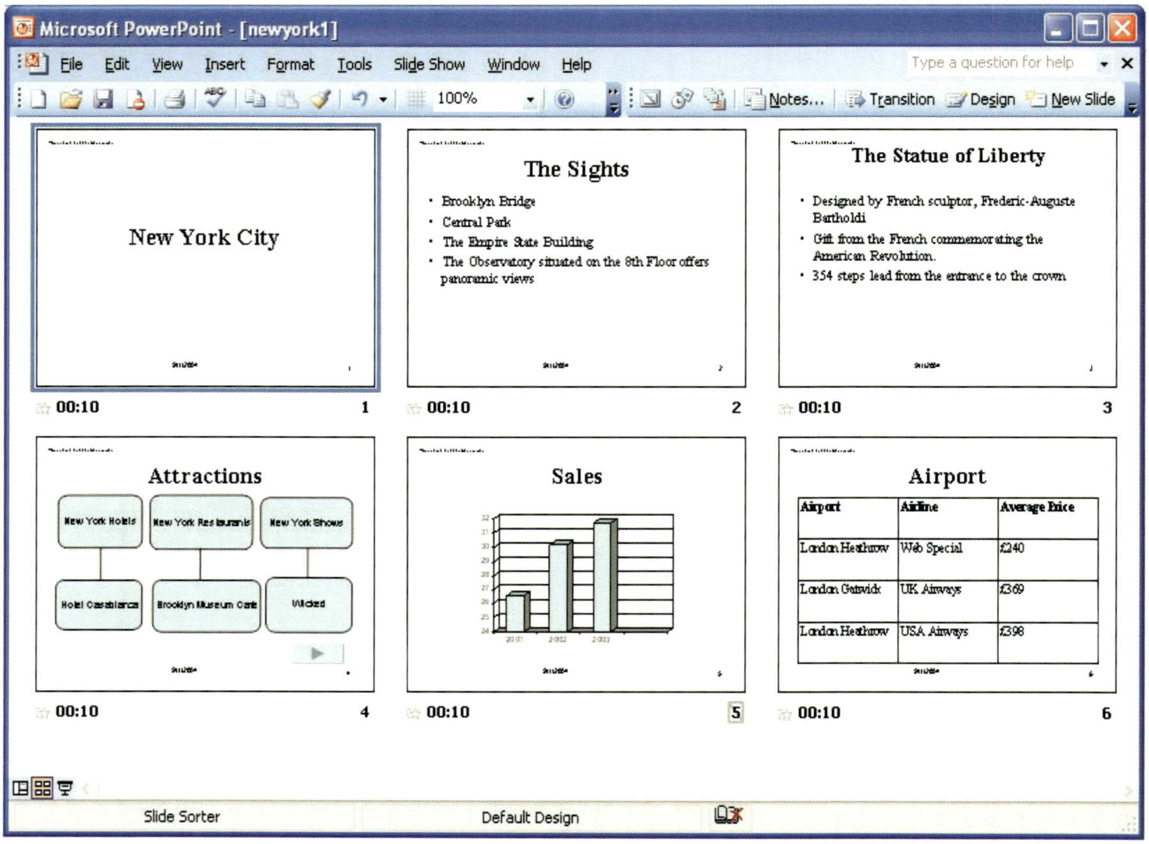

Graphics

Importing and editing graphics and Clip Art

In this section you will import graphics that Microsoft provided with the Office package or those from any appropriate Clip Art gallery.

- Getting started
- Creating text slides
- Changing the look of slides
- Preparing on-screen presentations
- Charts
- Graphics
  - **Importing graphics and Clip Art**
  - **Moving, duplicating and deleting graphics**
  - Resizing and cropping graphics
  - Exercise on Graphics
- Preparing and publishing presentations

Skill Builder **5.16**

1. Open the presentation *bears.ppt.*
2. Insert the supplied logo image *bears.jpg* in the bottom centre of slides 1, 2 and 3.
3. Ensure that all text is legible and the image has not superimposed any of the text.
4. Copy the image *bears.jpg* so that is displayed in the centre on slide 7.
5. Save the presentation as *bears.ppt* and close the file.

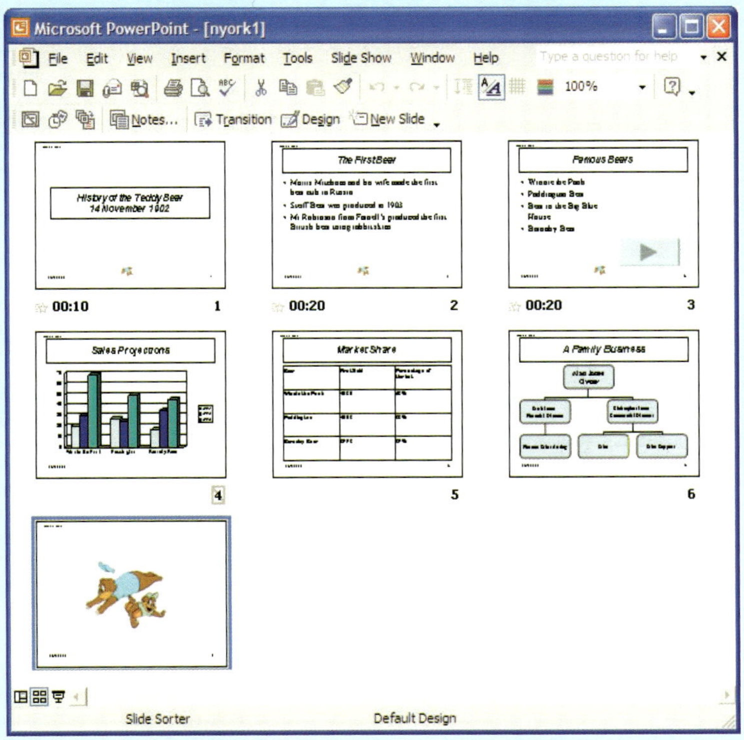

Resizing and cropping graphics

Getting started
Creating text slides
Changing the look of slides
Preparing on-screen presentations
Charts
Graphics
Preparing and publishing presentations
Importing graphics and Clip Art
Moving, duplicating and deleting graphics
Resizing and cropping graphics
Exercise on Graphics

To crop a graphic you will need the Picture toolbar. To display this, right-click on any toolbar and select **Picture** from the drop-down menu. Select the picture then click on the **Crop** tool on the Picture toolbar.

Skill Builder **5.17**

1 Open the presentation *bears.ppt* and crop the larger bear from the image in the centre of slide 7 ensuring that the smaller bear is still displayed.

2 Cut the bear from slides 1, 2 and 3 and paste this into the footer area of the master slide. Resize the image so that it becomes very small but still visible.

3 Save the presentation as *bears.ppt* and close the file.

Your presentation should be similar to this

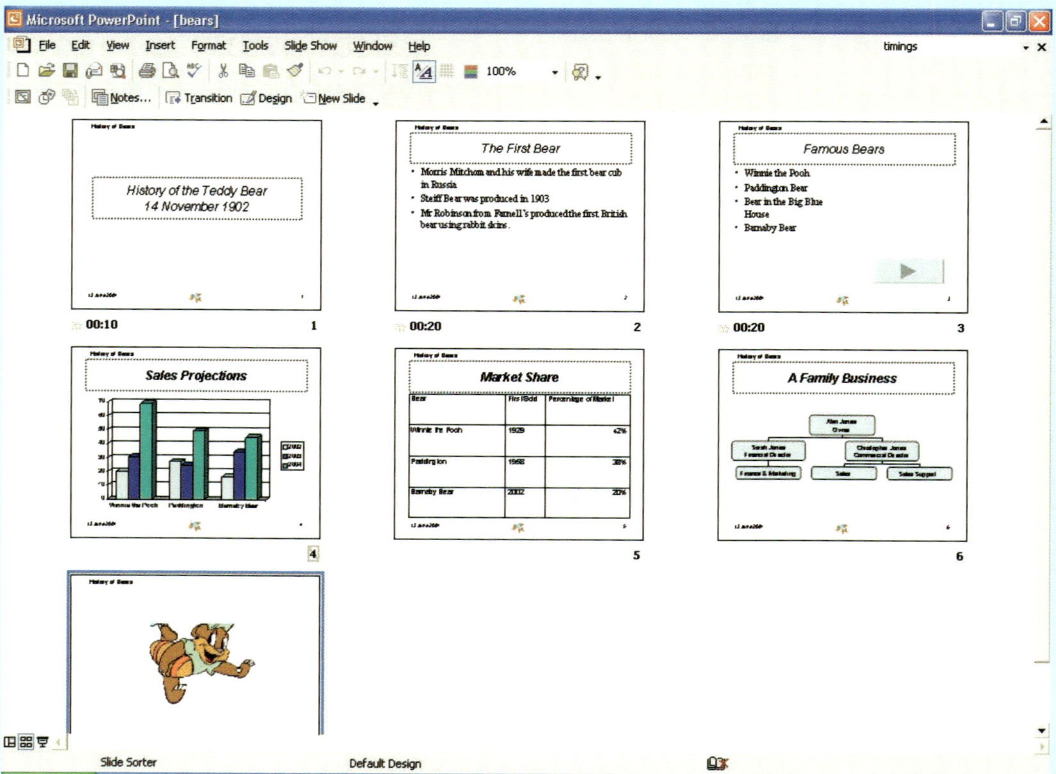

Preparing and publishing presentations

Replacing text

In a presentation you can use the **Replace** dialogue box if you want to change a word in a presentation.

- Getting started
- Creating text slides
- Changing the look of slides
- Preparing on-screen presentations
- Charts
- Graphics
- Preparing and publishing presentations
  - **Checking your presentation for spelling errors**
  - **Using the Replace dialogue box**
  - Creating speaker's notes and handouts
  - Printing slides
  - Printing a screen shot of a slide
  - Exercise on Preparing and publishing presentations
  - Task on Preparing and publishing presentations

Skill Builder 5.18

1 Open the presentation *bears.ppt*.

2 Find the word **sales** and replace with the word **selling**.

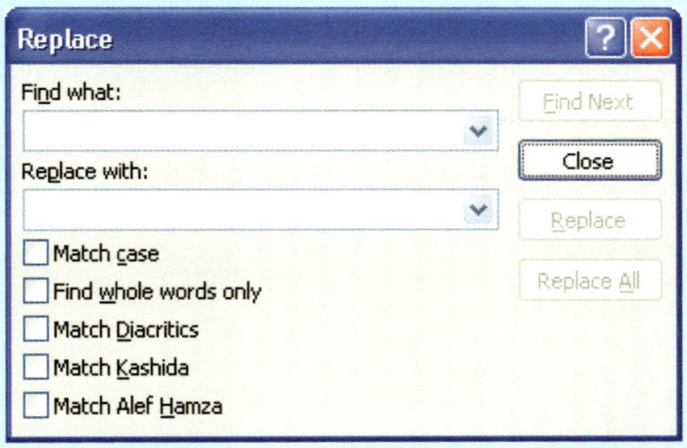

3 Ensure that any of the titles that have been changed have retained the correct case.

4 Close the file without saving the changes.

Creating speaker's notes

In the following Skill Builder you will add speaker's notes to the existing presentation. Speaker's notes help you when making the presentation and can act as a reminder.

- Getting started
- Creating text slides
- Changing the look of slides
- Preparing on-screen presentations
- Charts
- Graphics
- Preparing and publishing presentations
  - Checking your presentation for spelling errors
  - Using the Replace dialogue box
  - **Creating speaker's notes and handouts**
  - Printing slides
  - Printing a screen shot of a slide
  - Exercise on Preparing and publishing presentations
  - Task on Preparing and publishing presentations

Skill Builder 5.19

1 Open the presentation *bears.ppt* and add the following notes to the *Famous Bears* slide as speaker's notes by clicking in the Notes Pane at the bottom of this slide.

Winnie the Pooh was created by A A Milne who has always acknowledged that his wife, Daphne, and his young son, Christopher Robin, inspired him to write the poems and stories when the very young Christopher Robin was introduced to a bear at the London Zoo.

2 Save the presentation as *bears.ppt* and close the file.

Your solution should be similar to this

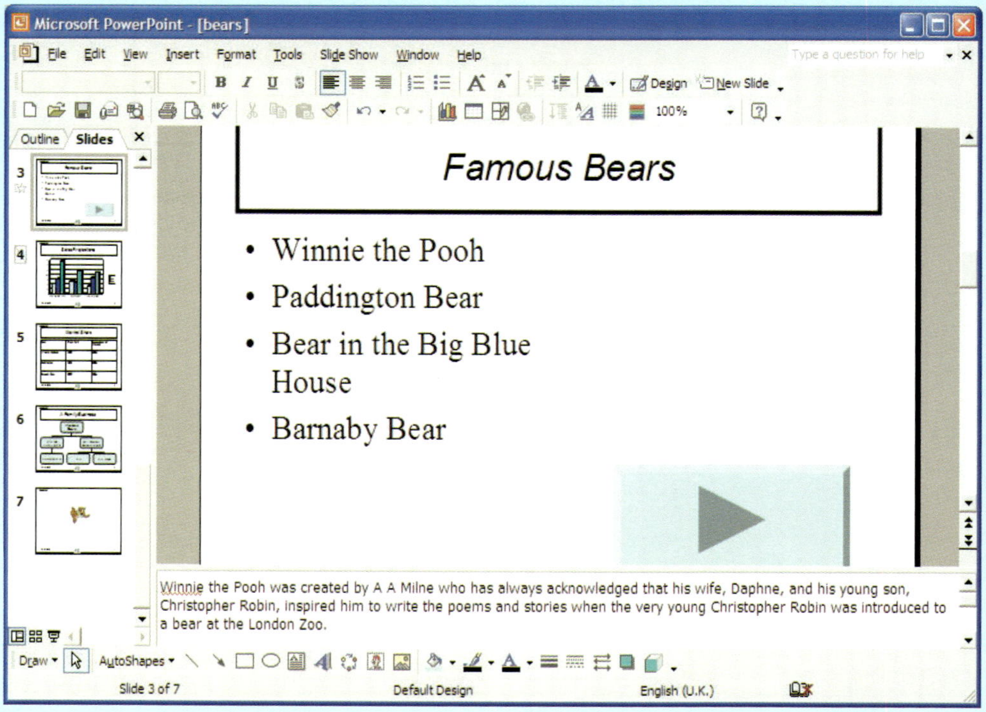

Printing slides and screen shots

You can print all slides on separate sheets of paper, or print handouts, notes pages or outline view.

In the CLAIT Plus assessment you will be required to produce a screen print showing the transitions, builds and timings you have applied to the slides.

- Getting started
- Creating text slides
- Changing the look of slides
- Preparing on-screen presentations
- Charts
- Graphics
- Preparing and publishing presentations
  - Checking your presentation for spelling errors
  - Using the Replace dialogue box
  - Creating speaker's notes and handouts
  - **Printing slides**
  - **Printing a screen shot of a slide**
  - Exercise on Preparing and publishing presentations
  - Task on Preparing and publishing presentations

Skill Builder **5.20**

1. Open the presentation *bears.ppt* and produce a printout of all slides on single sheets of paper.
2. Produce a separate printout of handouts showing 3 slides per page.
3. Produce a printout in Outline view. Do not show the hidden slide (check that there is no tick in the **Print hidden slides** box in the **Print** dialogue box).
4. Open the presentation *bears.ppt* and show the presentation on screen in Slide Sorter View. Press the **[Alt]** and **[Prt Sc]** keys.
5. Open Word and paste the screen capture into your Word document.
6. Save the file as *scpr1* and close Word.
7. Save the presentation and close it.

Your screen shot should be similar to this

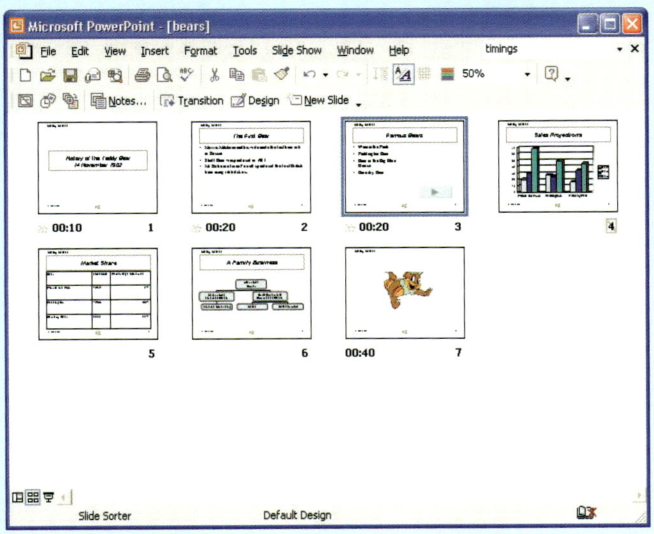

Mini Assignment 5.3

1 Open the presentation *newyork1.ppt.*

2 Import *nyork.jpg* as the logo in the top right-hand corner of the master slide, according to the house style.

House Style for Logo

Position	Additional information
Top right	Must not superimpose any text. Keep in proportion when resizing

3 Add the speaker's notes from the notes file *nspeak.txt* as indicated in the source file.

4 Print one copy of the slides.

5 Print one copy as handouts showing 6 slides per page.

6 Produce screen shots showing the animations and timings you have applied.

Your screen shots should be similar to these

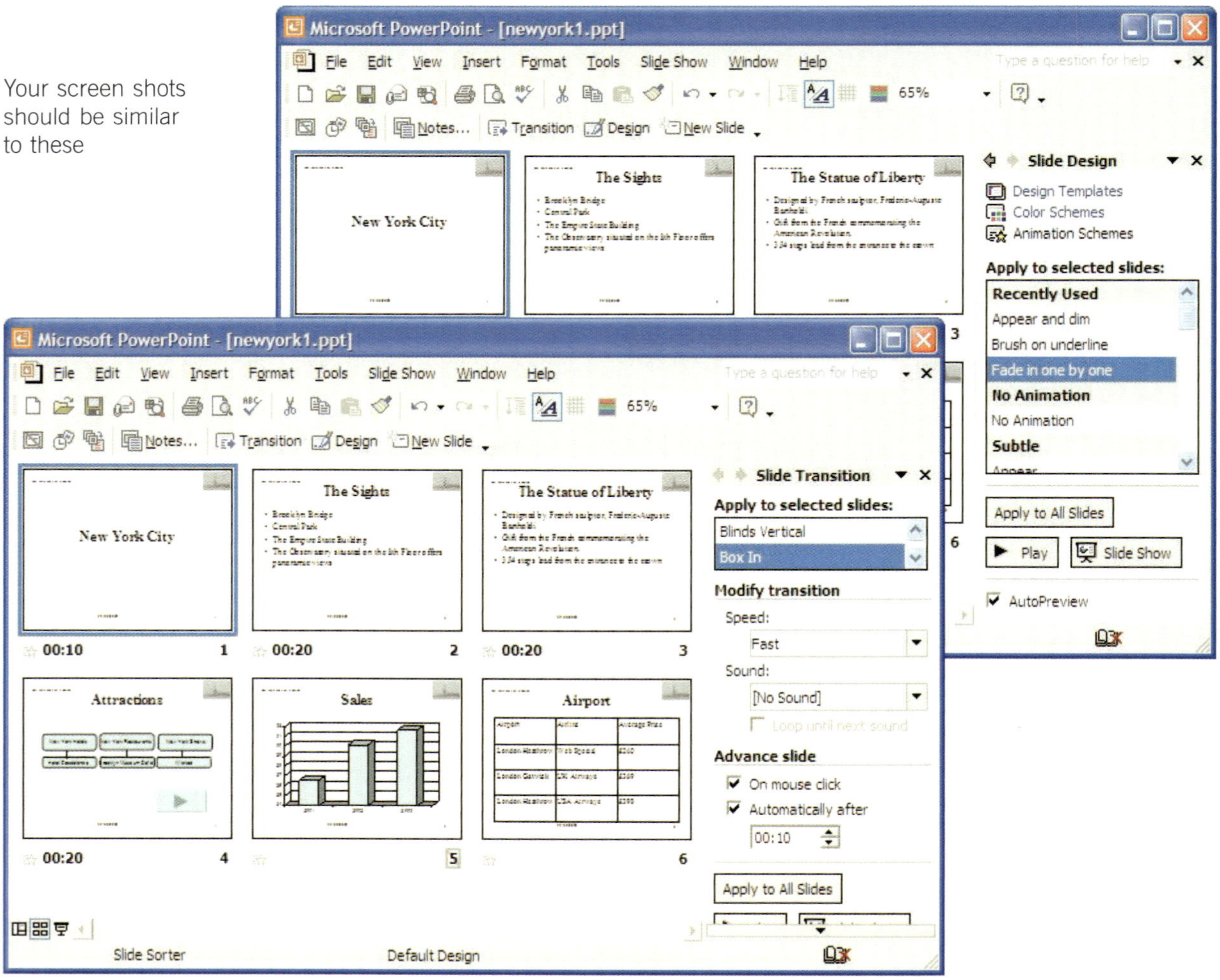

Unit 8

E-COMMUNICATIONS

Microsoft Outlook® allows you to communicate with others electronically. With e-mail you can quickly mail your colleagues with information, requests or send file attachments. Your recipients can read and respond to any requests quickly and efficiently without having to wait for printed copy to arrive in the post. You can send photos to friends or relatives anywhere in the world in a few seconds.

Outlook also allows you to control your calendar and manage appointments. You can create appointments, recording and displaying their time, location and other details. They can be recurring, e.g. weekly, or one-offs. You can even add files to calendar entries so that you are prepared for each meeting.

- Create, manage and integrate files
- Spreadsheets
- Databases
- Presentation graphics
- E-communications

Throughout this chapter you will be asked to open files that are supplied in the Resource Bank. They can be found on the Resource Bank CD or in the folder which your tutor may have set up for use with this course.

Getting started with e-mail

What is e-mail

Outlook is a software package which allows you to manage your e-mail, keep notes and add items to the calendar. The software allows you to set recurring appointments and reminders.

- Getting started with e-mail
  - What is e-mail?
  - Introducing Outlook
  - Customising the Inbox
  - Using Microsoft Office Help
  - Closing the application
  - Exercise on Getting started with e-mail
- Sending and receiving messages
- More about e-mail
- Good practice with e-mail
- Using Outlook to manage your time
- Printing from Outlook

Skill Builder **8.1**

1. Open Microsoft Outlook and ensure that **Inbox** is selected in the Folder list.
2. Open your Inbox and check for any new messages.
3. Customise the current view by adding the *Read* field to the display.
4. Close Microsoft Outlook.

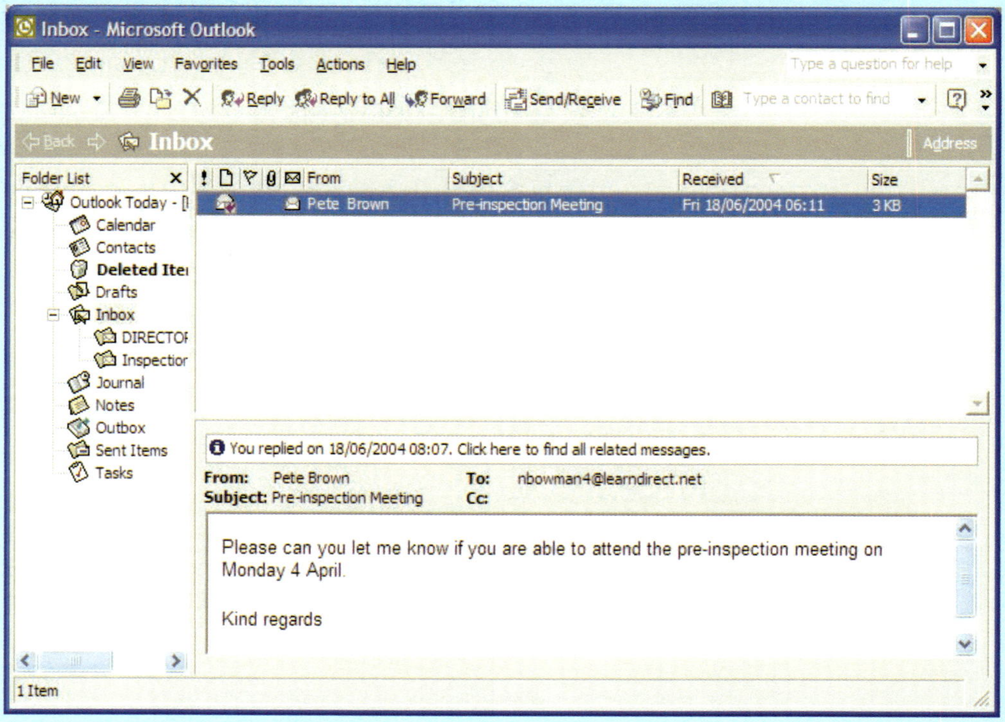

Sending and receiving messages

Creating and sending messages

In this Skill Builder you will create a new e-mail message and send it to our special mailbox for receiving messages from students.

- Getting started with e-mail
- Sending and receiving messages
  - Creating and sending messages
  - Reading received e-mail
  - Replying to messages
  - Forwarding messages
  - Editing messages
  - Working with e-mail addresses
  - Exercise on Sending and receiving messages
  - Task on Sending and receiving messages
- More about e-mail
- Good practice with e-mail
- Using Outlook to manage your time
- Printing from Outlook

Skill Builder 8.2

1 Open Microsoft Outlook.

2 Create the following names and addresses in your address book:

Name:	Alison Sullivan	David Jones
Job Title:	Marketing Manager	Developer
Address:	Electric Paper Gayton Road Harrow Middlesex HA1 2XU	Electric Paper No.1 Deansgrange Business Park Blackrock Co. Dublin
E-mail:	asullivan@electricpaper.ie	djones@electricpaper.ie

3 Create a mailing list named *managers* and add the two e-mail addresses to the mailing list. Remember: select **Address Book > New**, then enter the name of the group, and click **Select Members...** to add the members.

Your solution should be similar to this

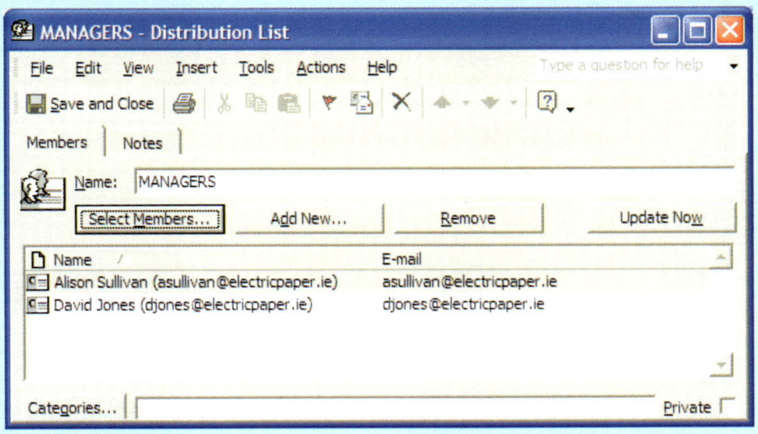

4 Create a new e-mail message to Alison Sullivan.

5 In the **To:** box key in the e-mail address of Alison Sullivan.

6 In the **Subject:** box key in the subject Pre-Inspection Meeting.

7 In the body of the message key in the following text:

Dear Alison

I have confirmation from the lead inspector that they will be arranging a pre-inspection meeting on Monday 4 April at 0900 hours in the company boardroom.

The lead inspector will be accompanied by her team which will include a specialist inspector in Business Management and IT and a specialist inspector looking at the company recording systems.

I would be grateful if you could provide me with a suitable agenda for the meeting.

Regards

Centre Co-ordinator

8 Make sure that the e-mail option to save copies of messages in *Sent Items* folder is turned on.

9 Click the **Send** button.

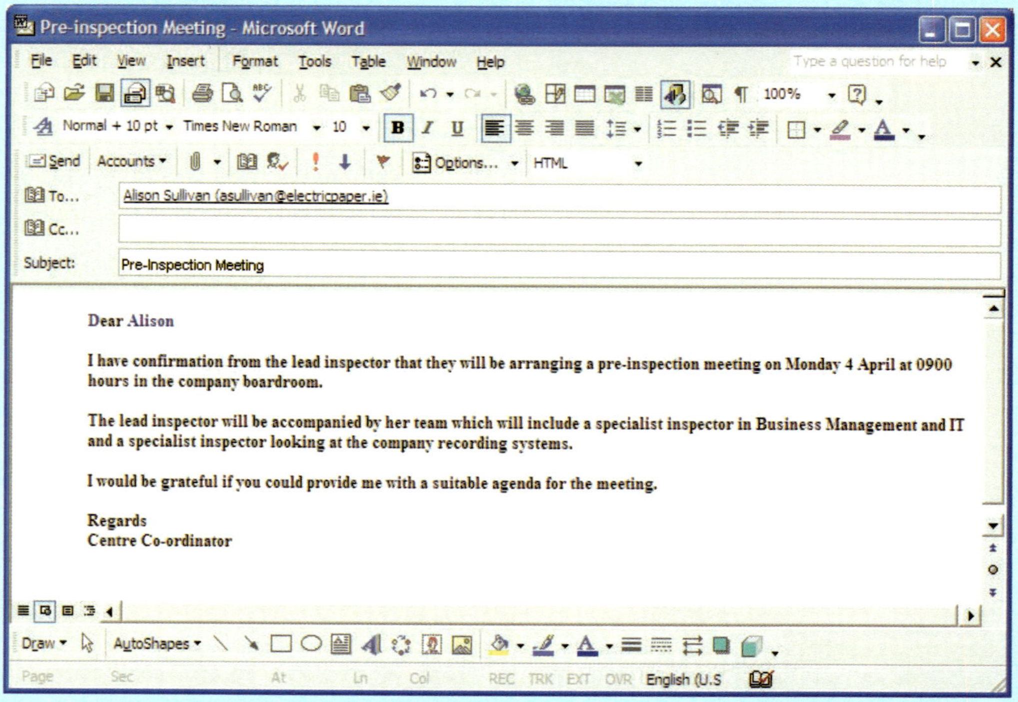

Replying to messages

Ask your tutor to send you a message regarding the pre-inspection meeting so that you are able to do the next Skill Builder. The e-mail will contain file attachments which will be used in the following section.

- Getting started with e-mail
- Sending and receiving messages
  - Creating and sending messages
  - Reading received e-mail
  - **Replying to messages**
  - Forwarding messages
  - Editing messages
  - Working with e-mail addresses
  - Exercise on Sending and receiving messages
  - Task on Sending and receiving messages
- More about e-mail
- Good practice with e-mail
- Using Outlook to manage your time
- Printing from Outlook

Skill Builder **8.3**

1 Open your Inbox in Outlook.

2 Click the **Send/Receive** button to check for any new messages.

3 You should have received a message from your tutor with the subject heading Pre-inspection Meeting.

4 Double-click on the message to open it.

5 Click on the **Reply** button to reply to this message.

6 Add a BCC to copy the message to the *managers* mailing list.

7 Key in the following text:

I confirm that I am able to attend the pre-inspection meeting which is to be held on Monday 4 April.
Kind regards

8 Click **Send** and ensure that a copy is saved in the *Sent Items* folder.

Your solution should be similar to this

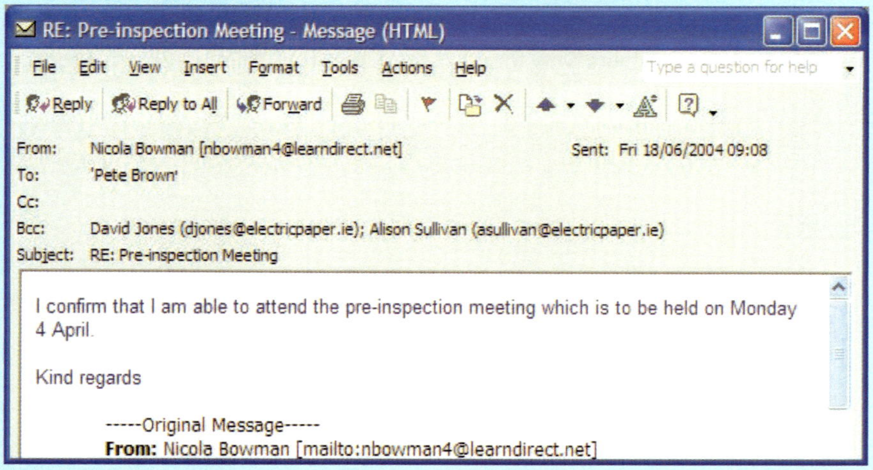

Sending and receiving messages

This gives further practice in sending and receiving e-mails.

- Getting started with e-mail
- Sending and receiving messages
  - Creating and sending messages
  - Reading received e-mail
  - Replying to messages
  - Forwarding messages
  - Editing messages
  - Working with e-mail addresses
  - Exercise on Sending and receiving messages
  - Task on Sending and receiving messages
- More about e-mail
- Good practice with e-mail
- Using Outlook to manage your time
- Printing from Outlook

Skill Builder 8.4

1 Open Outlook and create a message to the following two e-mail addresses:

asullivan@electricpaper.ie djones@electricpaper.ie

2 Type in the Subject line: Testing Message.

3 Key in and send the following message:

Dear All

I have been informed that some of my messages have been returned and am just checking that this e-mail is working.

Please reply to this message to enable me to check that the ISP is working correctly and I have the correct e-mail addresses.

4 Customise the view so that unread messages are displayed in the Inbox.

5 Change your e-mail settings so that the original message is not included with your reply.

6 Send a response to one person who has sent you a message and include the text:

Thank you for your message. I will deal with your request shortly.

7 Spell check this message.

8 Forward a message you have received to another member of your class using the appropriate Outlook toolbar button.

9 Open the Address Book. Check the names, addresses and e-mail addresses of your contacts and delete any contacts that you no longer need.

10 Close Microsoft Outlook.

More about e-mail

Using personal signatures

You can create a 'signature' – a short text file – and have it added automatically to any e-mails that you send.

- Getting started with e-mail
- Sending and receiving messages
- More about e-mail
  - **Using personal signatures**
  - Sending and receiving files with e-mail
  - Marking your messages
  - Exercise on More about e-mail
  - Task on More about e-mail
- Good practice with e-mail
- Using Outlook to manage your time
- Printing from Outlook

Skill Builder **8.5**

1. Open the **Tools** menu and select **Options**. Go to the **Mail Format** tab and click the **Signatures...** button to reach the **Create Signature** dialogue box.
2. Click **New...** and type in:

   Your name

   Your centre number

   Administrative Assistant
3. Check the signature and edit as necessary.

Your solution should be similar to this

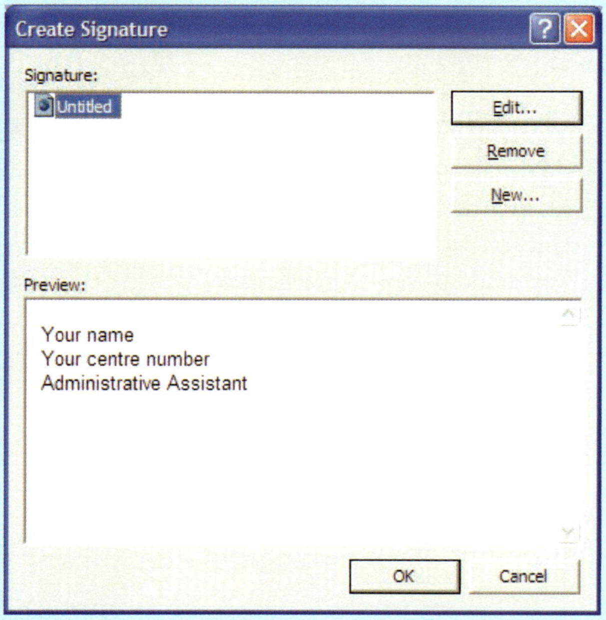

Sending and receiving files with e-mail

In the following Skill Builder you will create a new e-mail message and attach files which have been sent to you by your tutor.

- Getting started with e-mail
- Sending and receiving messages
- More about e-mail
  - Using personal signatures
  - **Sending and receiving files with e-mail**
  - **Marking your messages**
  - Exercise on More about e-mail
  - Task on More about e-mail
- Good practice with e-mail
- Using Outlook to manage your time
- Printing from Outlook

Note: Tutors will need to send students an e-mail with the subject 'Pre-Inspection Meeting', attaching the files *agenda*, *notes* and *team*. If you are working alone, send yourself the e-mail, attaching the files from the Resource Bank.

Skill Builder **8.6**

1. Locate the message from your tutor with the subject *Pre-Inspection Meeting*.
2. There are three file attachments with this message: *Agenda*, *notes*, *team*. Save the files in a convenient folder, e.g. *My Documents*.
3. Create a new e-mail message and address it to David Jones.
4. Key in the Subject box: Pre-Inspection Meeting Documentation.
5. Key in the following body text:

   With reference to the pre-inspection meeting to be held on Monday 4 April 2005 I have pleasure in enclosing a draft agenda together with notes relating to the format of the inspection. I also attach a copy of a document which shows details of members of the inspection team which I would be grateful if you could peruse to identify any areas of concern.

   A company pre-inspection meeting will be held on Monday 29 March in the Company Boardroom at 0930 hours to discuss the attached documentation.

   Kind regards

   Training Administrator
6. Attach the three files, *Agenda*, *notes*, *team*.
7. Send the message ensuring that a copy is saved in your *Sent Items* folder.

Your solution should be similar to this

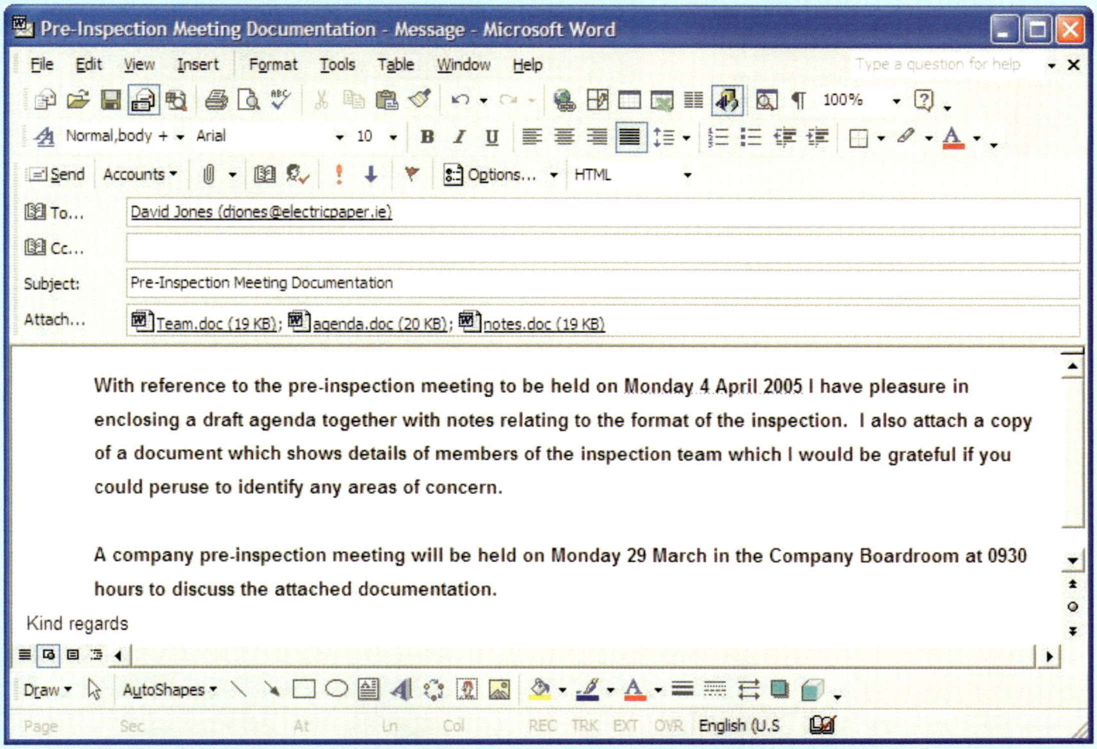

Good practice with e-mail

Managing your e-mail

In this Skill Builder you will create a new folder to store your e-mail messages – it is good practice to store messages away from your Inbox. This allows you to keep copies of messages that relate to specific topics or from specific people separately, and also reduces the number of messages held in your Inbox.

- Getting started with e-mail
- Sending and receiving messages
- More about e-mail
- Good practice with e-mail
  - Managing your e-mail
  - Setting rules for incoming messages
  - E-mail tips
  - Exercise on Good practice with e-mail
- Using Outlook to manage your time
- Printing from Outlook

Skill Builder 8.7

1 Click on **Inbox** in the **Folder List** and select **File > New > Folder**.

2 Key in the folder name: Inspection.

3 Click **OK**.

You should now be able to see the folder called *Inspection*.

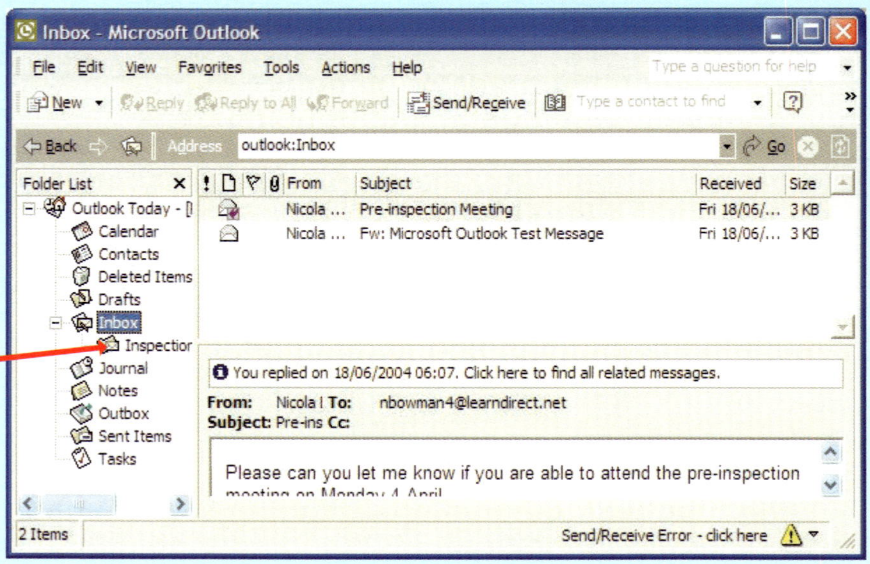

Your new folder should be here

Setting rules for incoming messages

In Outlook you can filter e-mail messages to be moved automatically into other folders. This is a good way of managing your Inbox, especially if you receive a large number of messages from either one person or relating to a specific topic.

- Getting started with e-mail
- Sending and receiving messages
- More about e-mail
- Good practice with e-mail
  - Managing your e-mail
  - **Setting rules for incoming messages**
  - E-mail tips
  - Exercise on Good practice with e-mail
- Using Outlook to manage your time
- Printing from Outlook

Skill Builder **8.8**

1. Create a new folder named *epaper*.
2. Move the *epaper* folder onto the Outlook shortcuts bar.
3. Create a new rule so that all messages from *asullivan@electricpaper.ie* are moved into the *epaper* folder.
4. Produce screen prints showing the new folder and the rule.
5. Close Outlook.

Your solution should be similar to this

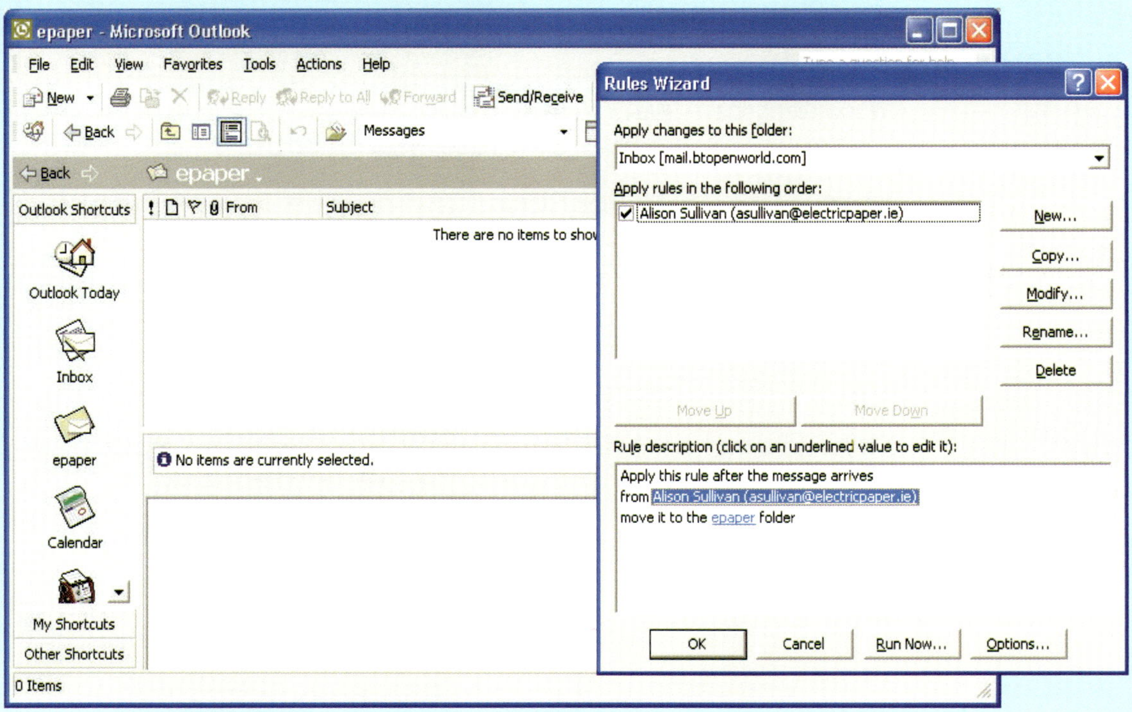

Mini Assignment 8.1

You are employed as an administrative assistant working with the company New York Today. You use e-mail software to send and receive communications.

Company policy for the use of e-mail and organiser software states that:

- all incoming e-mail messages must be moved into a dedicated archive folder
- all outgoing messages must be saved and printed showing header details, including sender, recipient(s), date and subject
- the default priority for outgoing messages must be set to normal
- all outgoing messages must close with your company approved e-mail signature, in the form:

  Your name

  Your centre number

  Administrative Assistant, New York Today

- all printouts of calendar, notes pages and to-do task lists include your personal details, i.e. name and centre number
- printouts should economise on paper where possible.

1 Two new Administrative Officers have been recruited to New York Today. Update your contacts list to show the amended contact details:

Name:	Mrs Alison Sullivan
Job title:	Administrative Officer
Work address:	21 Claypath, Durham
Postcode:	DH1 3LE
Work telephone:	0911 245189
E-mail:	asullivan@electricpaper.ie

Name:	Mr David Jones
Job title:	Administrative Officer
Work address:	The Watermill, Wakefield Road, Rotherham
Postcode:	RM5 7PQ
Work telephone:	01543 6232456
E-mail:	djones@electricpaper.ie

2 Create an e-mail distribution list named *Officer* holding the e-mail addresses of these two contacts.

3 Within your e-mail system create a dedicated archive folder to hold the messages from the Company Director. Call this folder *Director*.

4 Create and store your company-approved e-mail signature.

Using Outlook to manage your time

Personal information management

In this Skill Builder you will use the Personal information management software (PIM) in Outlook to manage calendar entries for the Software Developers.

- Getting started with e-mail
- Sending and receiving messages
- More about e-mail
- Good practice with e-mail
- Using Outlook to manage your time
  - Personal information management
  - Working with the Outlook calendar
  - Using tasks
  - Creating notes
  - Exercise on Using Outlook to manage your time
  - Task on Using Outlook to manage your time
- Printing from Outlook

Skill Builder **8.9**

1 Open Outlook and select the Calendar option from the Outlook shortcuts bar.

2 Change the Start time and End time of your working day to:

Start time: 09:30

End time: 17:30

3 Leave the other options unchanged.

4 Click **OK** then **OK** again.

It is recommended that you produce a screen print at this point to show that you have amended the times of the working day.

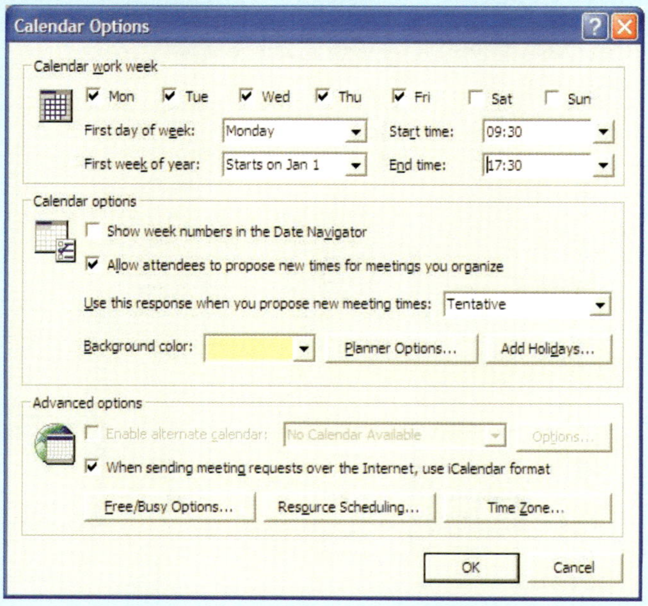

Working with the Outlook calendar

You will now create the following appointments – remember to access the relevant date and key in the relevant entry and the correct time:

- Getting started with e-mail
- Sending and receiving messages
- More about e-mail
- Good practice with e-mail
- Using Outlook to manage your time
  - Personal information management
  - **Working with the Outlook calendar**
  - Using tasks
  - Creating notes
  - Exercise on Using Outlook to manage your time
  - Task on Using Outlook to manage your time
- Printing from Outlook

Skill Builder **8.10**

1 Enter the following appointments and meetings into the Calendar.

Day	Start Time	Duration	Memo/Description	Repeating/recurring
Monday	10 am	1 hour	Pre-Inspection Meeting (Company Boardroom)	Weekly
	2 pm	30 mins	Update meeting on company quality procedures	No
Tuesday	9.30 am	1 hour	Meeting with printers re: review of contract	No
	1 pm	2 hours	Review with Accountant re: finance workshop	No
Thursday	10 am	1 hour	Team briefing (Oxford Room)	No
Friday	12.30 pm	2 hours	Working lunch re: new training programme	No

Your solution should be similar to this

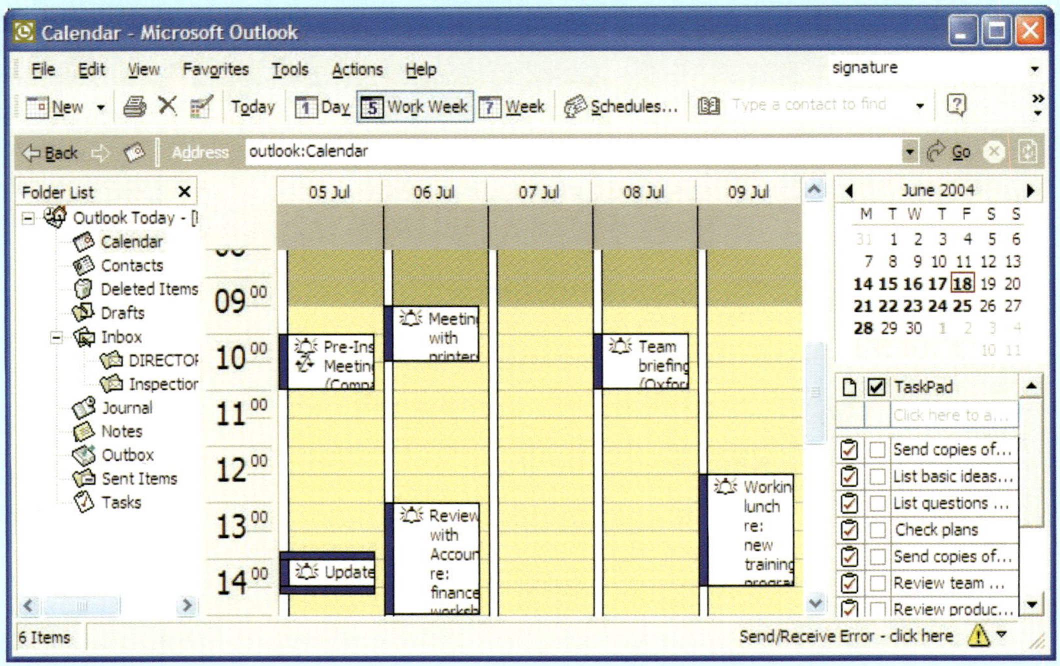

Using tasks

The tasks function allows you to prioritise your workload by due date. You can 'tick off' tasks as you complete them.

- Getting started with e-mail
- Sending and receiving messages
- More about e-mail
- Good practice with e-mail
- Using Outlook to manage your time
  - Personal information management
  - Working with the Outlook calendar
  - **Using tasks**
  - Creating notes
  - Exercise on Using Outlook to manage your time
  - Task on Using Outlook to manage your time
- Printing from Outlook

Skill builder 8.11

1 Enter the following To Do tasks:

Start	Memo/Description	Due by
Monday	Review pre-inspection documentation	Monday
Tuesday	Review objectives of finance presentation	Tuesday
Wednesday	Prepare documentation for meeting re: training programme	Friday

Your solution should be similar to this

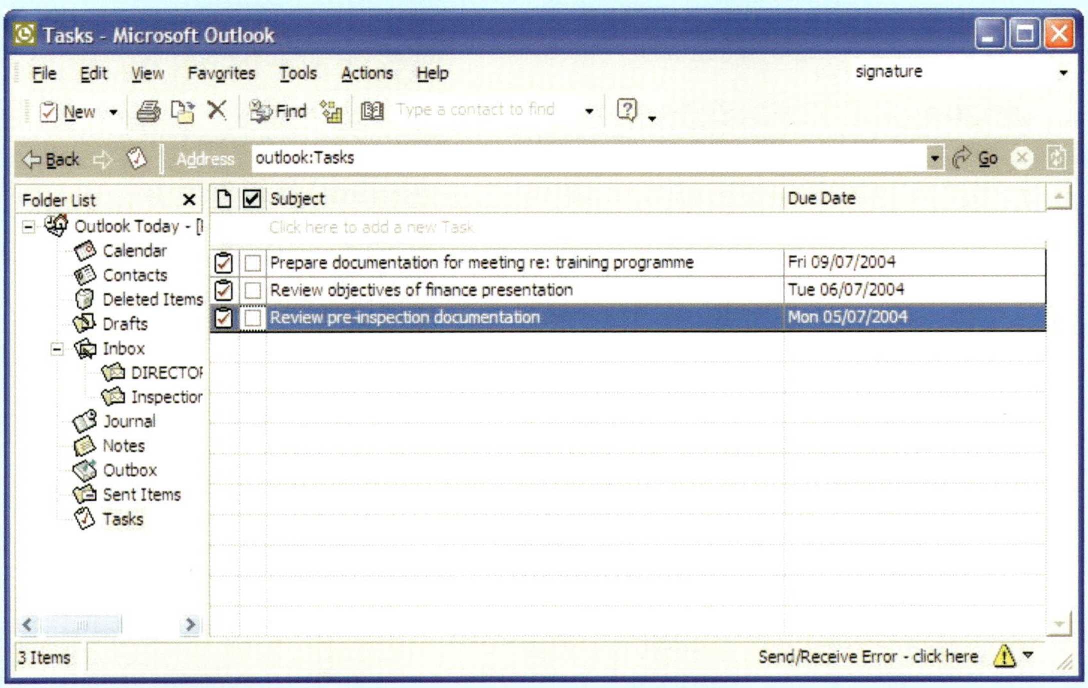

Printing from Outlook

Printing e-mails, contact details and calendar items

In this Skill Builder we will print out copies of the e-mails, entries in your Address Book and calendar items.

- Getting started with e-mail
- Sending and receiving messages
- More about e-mail
- Good practice with e-mail
- Using Outlook to manage your time
- Printing from Outlook
  - **Printing e-mails**
  - **Printing contact details**
  - **Printing calendar items**
  - Exercise on Printing from Outlook

Skill Builder **8.12**

1 Print one copy of each of the e-mails that you have sent and received.

2 Access the Address Book entries for A Sullivan, D Jones and Manager and print one copy of each entry in memo style.

3 Print one copy of the group you have created in your Address Book.

4 Print one copy of your calendar items and copies of your To Do lists.

5 Make the following amendments to your calendar items:

The Update Meeting on Company Procedures on Monday needs to be extended to 2 hours and will now start at 2.30 pm on Monday.

You have decided to attend a conference on electronic learning materials at the National Centre, Oxford on Wednesday. Add this all-day appointment.

6 Print off a revised copy of your calendar and close Outlook securely.

Your solution should be similar to this

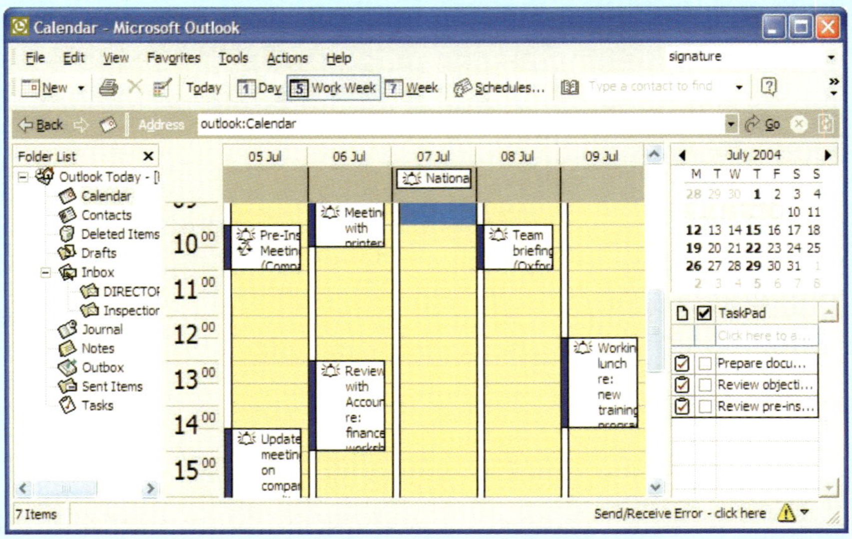

Mini Assignment 8.2

You use Personal information management (PIM) software to help you organise your working week and to keep details of contacts.

1 Open Outlook and change the Start time and End time of your working day to:

Start time: 09:15

End time: 17:15

2 Create the following appointments (using the dates for the next working week) – remember to access the relevant date and key in the relevant entry and the correct time:

Day	Start Time	Duration	Memo/Description	Repeating/recurring
Monday	9.45 am	1 hour	Press release meeting	Weekly
	2 pm	30 mins	Update meeting on monthly targets	No
Tuesday	10.15 am	1 hour	Meeting with printers re: new leaflets	No
	1 pm	1 hour	Review with accountant re: monthly budgets	No
Wednesday				
Thursday	9.30 am	1 hour	Weekly team briefing (Cambridge Room)	No
Friday	12.30 pm	2 hours	Working lunch re: new attractions	No

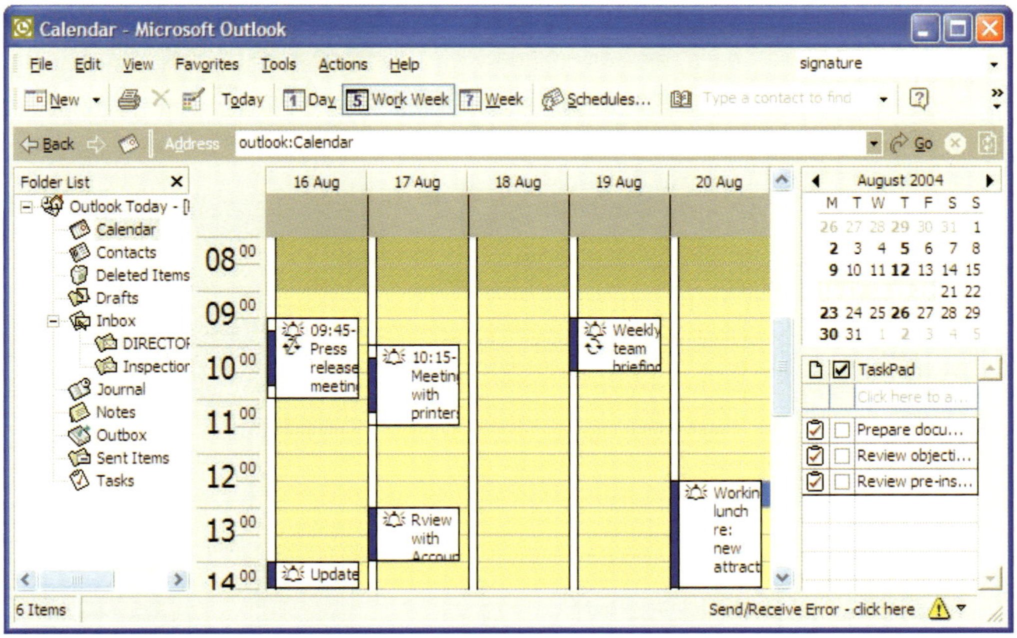

3 Enter the following To Do tasks:

Start	Memo/Description	Due by
Monday	Review new leaflet	Monday
Tuesday	Review monthly targets	Tuesday
Wednesday	Prepare documentation for meeting re: budgets	Friday

Your To Do list should be similar to this

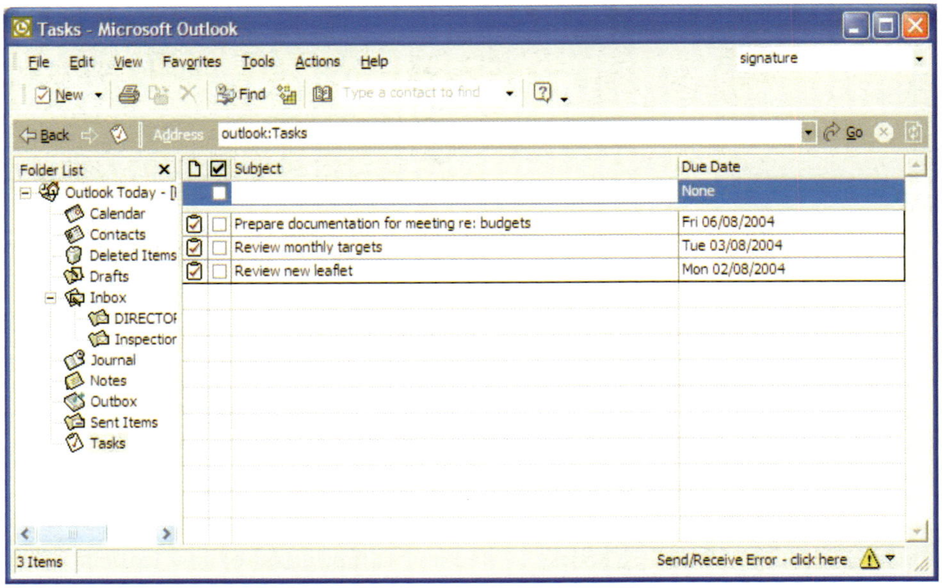

4 Make the following amendments to your calendar items:

The Press Release Meeting needs to be extended to 2 hours and will now start at 10 am.

You have decided to attend a conference at the National Centre, Cambridge on Wednesday (all day) which is concerned with electronic learning materials. Add this new all-day appointment to your diary.

5 Print off a copy of your revised calendar and close Outlook securely.

Your solution should be similar to this

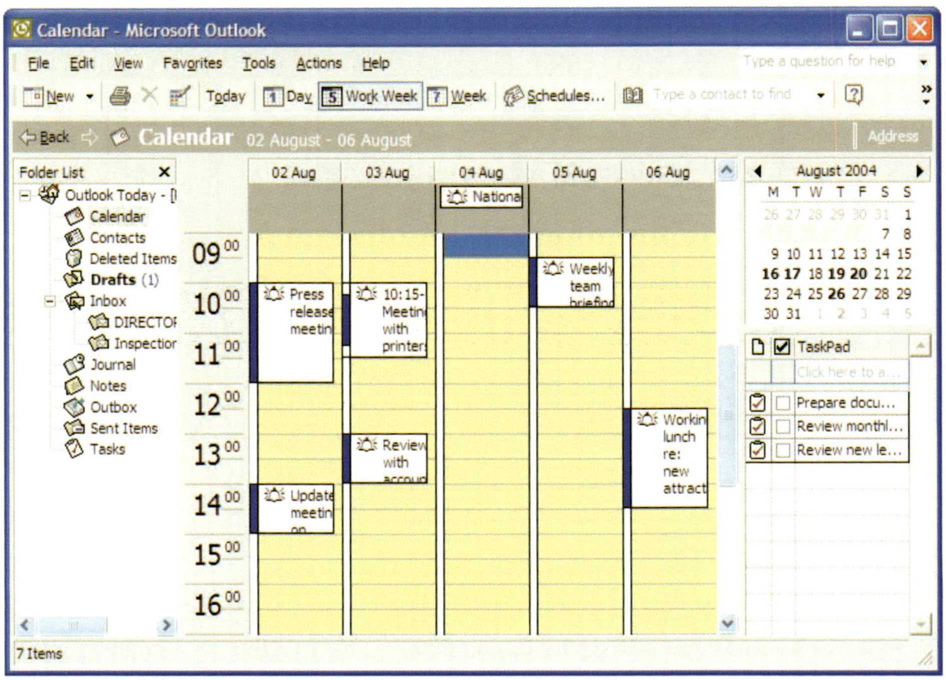